THE CHOICE IS YOURS: BALANCING SUCCESS AS WIFE, MOM, AND ENTREPRENEUR

Joni Wolfswinkel

"Be the heroine of your life, not the victim."

— Nora Ephron

INTRODUCTION

"When you have to make a choice and don't make it, that is in itself a choice" — William James

Not long ago, a client asked me, "What was the turning point that made you who you are today?"

In other words, what was my *ah-ha moment*?

I had to think about it for a second. Like I did, you may be struggling to find your own *ah-ha moment*.

As women, we are often hard on ourselves. We're surrounded by so much negativity that we question our womanhood, our parenting skills, our status as wives, and our entrepreneurial skills. Society tells us, *you can't do all of that.*

But, I believe we are capable of anything we put our minds to. If we believe in ourselves, if we're confident of our abilities, we can do anything.

As a result of this constant barrage of negative messaging, we women feel like we have to be validated—like a parking ticket. We feel like we should be stamped with a seal of approval. But a rubber stamp will not make us great moms, wives, and entrepreneurs. Validation from anywhere outside ourselves will not transform us into great business partners, visionary leaders, and pathpaving pioneers.

If you're like I used to be, you thrive on the approval of others. You may feel like you need someone else to approve your life choices. You may want others' blessing on your parenting choices, or someone to tell you what you're doing wrong. Maybe you seek permission to follow your dreams. In other words, you're looking for *validation.*

I'll tell you right here at the beginning, true validation comes from within, not through the eyes of others.

That's why I wrote this book.

For me, writing this book serves three purposes:

1. I want to empower women entrepreneurs to overcome the limitations they place on themselves and rise above the expectations imposed by others. Self-limiting beliefs hold us back. It may be cliché, but you are living *your* journey. Dream big and reach for the stars!

2. I also want to give women an inside look at a success story in the making. I'll share early experiences from my life as a child growing up with severe health issues in a dysfunctional family, along with the life lessons that grew me into the successful, happy woman I became. I'll also share insights into my life as a wife to my wonderful husband Shawn, mom to two incredible children—Lucas and Mila—and CEO of one of the most powerful real estate businesses in Texas.

3. Finally, I hope you'll find in this story permission to ignore what others think. It's okay to fail. It's also okay to succeed. So consider permitting yourself the luxury of going against the instinct to listen to what people outside your inner circle say about you. You aren't trying to please anyone other than you and your loved ones.

I'm not an expert in personal development. I'm a student. A lifelong learner. This story represents my journey as a student sharing what I've learned so far along the way.

Why do we feel a need for validation? Why do we choose misery over happiness? Why do we listen to the demons in our heads, whose goal is to drag us down and steal our happiness?

These are the questions we might ask ourselves if we want to overcome the demons.

I've found that it comes down to fear. Fear is the great killer of happiness. The destroyer of success. The murderer of self-satisfaction. I started out in life believing the lies wrapped up in these fears, but I didn't let it win. You don't have to let it win either. (For a list of common fears and how to overcome them, see Appendix 1 at the back of the book.)

I listened to the negativity fed to me by others for a long time. I started to believe the put downs because I felt like everything had to be perfect. Sound familiar?

Let me tell you, friend, I'm living proof your life will never be perfect. Despite the obstacles, you can be happy and fulfilled. You can live the life of your dreams. (Appendix 3 offers tips on living life to the fullest.)

You see, when I was a child, there was never a dull moment in our household. I grew up in a broken home, with a spiral of abuse and addiction that kept my back against the proverbial wall. My father was a heroin addict; my brother was a meth addict. My parents divorced when I was two years old and I spent most of my childhood without my biological father in my life.

There were times when I found myself in uncomfortable, sometimes incredible, situations. On several occasions, law enforcement officers raided our home. When I was thirteen years old, my older brother Joey and I went for a car ride and ended up at a drug house. We were supposed to be going for ice cream.

On another occasion, one of Joey's drug deals went bad and we received threats: we would be the target of a drive-by shooting unless Joey paid some debt he owed.

For several weeks, we didn't go near the windows. I'd roll my computer desk to the hallway and do my homework before bedtime, then sleep there. We lived this way because the local police department wouldn't protect us. They told us to either stay in the hallway or get out of the house. We practically lived in the hallway after that.

That was my *ah-ha moment*.

My family life a complete mess, I knew there had to be a better way. I was determined not to become a drug addict, like my father and brother. I had to get away from that awful way of life. Someone was going to get killed and I didn't want to be the victim. If I worked hard, I reasoned, I could be successful.

I've had some traumatic experiences. But I'll say this: What I went through as a child helped mold me into who I am today. I can handle more pressure because I was put in those uncomfortable situations. It wasn't right, but my childhood taught me how to adapt to any circumstance. I'm a stronger person because of it.

Growing up the way I did taught me how to cope with fear. There were times when I was afraid but managed to push through. Later in life, I'd draw from these experiences to help overcome fear, to build my business, and to care for my family. (Appendix 8 discusses the importance of emotion management. Flip back to that appendix for some tips on how to manage your emotions in times of crisis.)

My husband Shawn is my biggest encourager. He often tells me he admires me for my strength of character. He reminds me that many women cannot handle the pressure of managing a successful business and a home life. Together, Shawn and I have worked against the odds to build a successful business and a happy family together.

We all have challenging moments in life, but those moments can become opportunities. Choosing to recognize the opportunities gave me the power to build my life into the one I wanted. We all have challenges.. I believe how we choose to deal with those moments determines our fate.

I chose to use those opportunities to better myself. I chose to believe that no matter how bad my childhood may have been, I was not going to be sucked into that destructive lifestyle of drug addiction. I was not going to use those experiences as an excuse to have a shitty life. I was going to have the best life I could possibly have. A different life than my brother, Joey, who ultimately chose death over life.

Don't get me wrong, I love Joey. I love my whole family. But the life we had then was hard. It didn't make sense most of the time. I didn't want that life for my future family, the one I have now. Today, I'm much stronger. As horrible as it sounds, I'm thankful I had to live through those experiences so I can appreciate the work it took to get to where I am.

Looking back, I'm really amazed that I got here. This book is about how I faced my demons. It's about how I fought them and won. It's not a pretty story, but it's *my* story. You have one of your own that you're still writing.

If you're a woman and you're struggling, I want to encourage you to keep going. You *can* control your destiny—by exercising your right of choice.

It's not about being perfect. It's about striving to be better than you were yesterday. What matters is that you're happy, your family is happy, and that you're having the time of your life. Following your dreams instead of trying to please the world. If you see your own *ah-ha moments* as opportunities, you can take control of your life and pave your own path.

Success and happiness await you when you do. That's what I hope you walk away with after reading my story.

THE CHOICE IS YOURS: PLAY THE HAND YOU WERE DEALT

"Life is not always a matter of holding good cards, but sometimes, playing a poor hand well." — Jack London

Like a natural tree, a family tree has roots. What I know of my roots can fit into a thimble, but here it is in a nutshell.

Grandpa was a hard-working mailman and a World War II veteran. Grandma was a stay-at-home mom. She worked at least as hard at raising my mom and her two siblings as Grandpa worked at delivering the mail. Grandpa retired from the postal service and became the school crossing guard when I was in elementary school.

A real patriot, Grandpa served his country well. He didn't complain. In fact, he received a Bronze Star for heroic achievement and meritorious service in a combat zone. He didn't talk about it much, but when he did, he'd get emotional. A few times, when he opened up to share a few stories of his time as a medic on the battlefield, it drove him to tears. And when the tears started, Grandpa quit talking.

War is hell, they say. When a man has to treat his wounded friends and live with the images of that trauma for the rest of his life, who wouldn't cry out loud? Thinking about it now, I get emotional, too.

As a younger woman, Grandma worked for a while as a waitress at a restaurant in Santa Fe. But I'll always remember her as a housewife. That was her true occupation. In those days—we're talking about mid-twentieth century here—that's what most women did. Catholic women, especially. Maybe a better word for that occupation is *homemaker*. Grandma certainly made a cozy home for her children and grandchildren.

As faithful Catholics, they were in church every Sunday. They didn't miss Mass without a good reason, and those were few and far between. As you may already guess, they were about as conservative as a Catholic family could have been. In fact, they made modern conservatives look liberal.

Mom was the only girl, though she acted like more of a boy than her brothers. From the earliest age, she had an independent streak wider than both my uncles combined. The three of them attended St. Michael's Catholic High School in Santa Fe.

To say Mom was "independent" is an understatement. She was the odd ball in the family, the black sheep. The family (including me as a child) would often jokingly accuse Grandma of fooling around with the milkman while Grandpa was away at war. That's how different Mom was from the rest of the family.

She was the epitome of a teenage free spirit. Outspoken, outgoing, and the first of her siblings to leave the nest. Her older brother, Anthony, lived at home until he married, well into his forties. And little brother Gerard was sickly. That meant she had to carry the family torch.

She never said so to me, but I knew Mom had trouble with structure and didn't like the strict conservative rules placed on her by her Catholic parents. She couldn't wait to leave home.

Meanwhile, a teenager wanting a "normal" life in that environment had to figure out how to get around the rules. That often meant keeping secrets. Mom had her share.

For starters, she had some girlfriends Grandma wouldn't approve of. They were a little rebellious, too. Mom also dated younger than she should have. Clandestinely, of course. Whatever the rule was, if she didn't like it, she broke it. That meant breaking curfew, dating boys when she wasn't supposed to, the whole works. That rebellious streak would eventually get her into trouble.

In effect, she had the same rules I later had when I lived with Grandma and Grandpa: Curfew at ten p.m. No sleep overs at friends' houses. Talking on the phone was limited. It was almost a blatant sheltering. When she was old enough, Mom was all too eager to get out on her own.

My grandparents had a message for her. According to Mom, they said something like, "If you're independent enough to move out on your own, you'll have to pay for it because we aren't giving you a dime."

And they didn't, either. Like good Catholics, they were true to their word.

She must have been determined because Mom was out of the house as soon as she graduated from high school. It was 1976, the height of feminism's second wave. Women's liberation was a national movement, the "fairer sex" had our own national magazine, and some states had legalized no-fault divorce (though New Mexico wouldn't legalize it until much later).

She and her two friends, Debbie and a girl Mom called "Gorda," had their minds made up that they were going to leave Santa Fe and move to Roswell, New Mexico. What the devil was in Roswell that attracted them so much is anyone's guess. All I could ever see was smelly old cow farms, space alien visitation mania, and a lack of decent work opportunities. To Mom, it meant independence.

Looking back, I realize I took after her a lot. You could never tell Mom she couldn't do what she wanted to do. She'd prove you wrong. Grandma and Grandpa telling her she couldn't survive on her own was motivation and encouragement.

Her brother, Anthony, in her parents' eyes, was a saint. To this day, that's what they call him. "Saint." He did everything he was supposed to do, right up to not leaving home until he took a wife. The Catholic way.

Mom's younger brother was diagnosed with leukemia at seventeen and my grandparents spent a lot of time caring for him. With their hands full, they didn't have the energy for a rebel child. It seemed like a kind of vicious circle. The more they babied Gerard, the more Mom rebelled. And the more she rebelled, the more time they spent looking after Gerard. They just didn't know how to handle the independent spirit Mom threw in their faces.

Perhaps Mom felt she wasn't getting the attention she deserved, since they spent so much time caring for Gerard. That could have

11

played into her rebellion. But her parents' response was, You'll never make it on your own.

That was like throwing gasoline on a fire.

Mom couldn't care less about space aliens and cow farms. I don't think she had a plan, other than leaving home. She wanted to hang out with friends. Chase independence. Freedom is its own reward, "just another word for nothing left to lose" as the popular song says. It amazes me to this day that she had the courage to go out on her own like that, at a time when women were barely recognized as human. That she secured a job, found her own place to live—in Roswell, of all places!

After a few months of looking for work, she met some other young ladies who, to this day, are still her friends. They worked at Levi Strauss & Co, the jeans manufacturer. She must have been desparate for work. After all, without a job, she wasn't likely to find an apartment. She knew nothing about sewing or making clothes. But there she was, a cog in the machine, one person of many on an assembly line, sewing pants together. A job was a job.

Soon after landing that job, she met Joseph, the man who would become my father. He also worked at Levi Strauss.

Like many relationships, theirs began with an introduction by mutual friends. Joseph hung out with those friends after work and, after a few nights, he was dating Mom. Because of her limited experience with dating in high school, Mom didn't know what to expect. She rushed into it too soon.

But she had her coveted freedom. No longer under the strict oversight of her parents, she leaped into the night life and its associated activities—drinking, smoking pot, parties. She spun out of control. She practically threw herself into a serious relationship with Joseph almost as soon as they met.

I've often jokingly asked her, What the heck did you ever see in him? She was one of those girls who liked the bad boy type. The "cool" guy type who likes to party all night and sleep all day. So I'd joke with her, but it really was half-joking. Seriously, I wanted to know what she saw in him.

She'd respond, I honestly don't know what I was thinking. It felt right at the time, she'd say. They had the same party animal friends, and that's how it happened. At least, that's what she wants me to believe.

My grandparents would never have approved of Joseph, had they been there. He was not the type of guy you brought home to meet your momma, that's for darn sure. Heavy drinking, late nights out, pot smoking. Those things were not Catholic values. But that was the lifestyle Mom picked up. And it didn't end up pretty.

Not long after beginning to date Joseph, she found herself pregnant. If you know about "hard core" Catholics, this did not go over well with Grandma and Grandpa. Even by conservative standards, they were old-fashioned. Having children outside of marriage is a major no-no. It came as a shock to them when Mom spilled the beans. Ultimately, it drove Mom and Joseph prematurely toward the marriage altar.

"Marriage was not the best decision." Those were her words, quoting Grandpa. She told me that Grandpa whispered in her ear as he walked her down the aisle, saying something like, "Berta, you don't have to marry this guy just because you're pregnant. We will support you no matter what. We want you to be happy."

I think he also had some regrets about being so strict on her as a child, especially since it drove her to some of the choices she made. So what's one more bad decision?

Joseph's parents were also Catholic, so that was a big driver. Bad decision, big driver. And Grandpa did his best to talk Mom out of it, all the way up to walking her down the aisle of Our Lady of Guadalupe Catholic Church where he was a faithful member.

Marriage is challenging enough for mature couples with a plan. It's impossible for couples with major challenges, like those that Mom and Joseph had. They weren't prepared for it at all. Early on, while Mom was pregnant, Joseph would come home drunk or high on marijuana. Then he would verbally abuse her. It started with simple name calling and led to other insults. You know, the light stuff.

Whatever she did, she just wasn't good enough to meet his unreasonable expectations. If she served something for dinner that wasn't to his liking, she was a lousy cook. If the house wasn't cleaned to his standards, she was a terrible homemaker. He put her down like she was a slave and he, the master. With every word, he let her know how far she fell short.

Then things got physical.

One night, he came home high and drunk. He'd had a few beers and some pot—a popular item on the cultural menu in those days. Mom had made dinner, but it wasn't up to his standards. Joseph went off. He had had so much to drink and smoke, he lost his head. When Mom mouthed back, Joseph grabbed her arms and squeezed.

Mom's version of the story goes something like this:

She pulled away, "Stop! That hurts."

"You're my wife, damnit! I have a right to expect dinner on time, and just the way I like it." As Mom tells it, it was difficult to tell if it was Joseph's masculine insecurity talking, or the booze and drugs. "It's your duty to make me happy," he demanded.

She started to talk and Joseph raised his hand. Mom shrunk back. The hand flew anyway, the back of it across her cheek and over her lips, cracking the top lip so it bled. She fell to the floor.

Mom said Joseph looked stunned, as if he was as surprised as she was. He ran out the door. His anger had got the best of him, it seemed, but it wouldn't be the last time.

If it happens once, it's easier to justify it the second time. When an immature, drug-addled young man feels powerless, he can quickly fall into being the abusive husband. Over time, he didn't think twice.

They weren't married long, of course, before my brother Joey was born. He was a handsome little guy. They were so proud of him. After all, he was the first born. And they spoiled him. He got what he wanted most of the time.

But it wasn't long before Joseph's temper grew hotter. It's not a shocker, really. How many marriages have started on shaky ground because an immature young couple made the leap and had children before they were ready emotionally, financially, and psychologically? Marrying someone just because you're pregnant with their child is a really bad decision. It strains the relationship from the start.

When things get difficult, stressors take over. Take an already bad situation—a young couple with immaturity issues, drug and alcohol abuse, a hot temper, the lifestyle changes that come with adjusting to marriage. Add the unexpected challenges that come with raising a baby. A bad situation turns into a nightmare. That's exactly what happened.

The financial responsibility of caring for a newborn, not to mention the emotional toll it takes on the unprepared parents is hard. On top of that, Mom and Joseph didn't know each other well. And Joseph wasn't ready to grow up.

Their arguments soon rose to a fevered pitch. If Joseph didn't get his way, he'd throw things and pound on doors. The stress of child rearing led him back into the party lifestyle. At times, he wouldn't come home at night. While Mom was home tending to Joey, Joseph was out drinking and carousing. In fact, he started drinking more heavily. Then he began to experiment with heroin. That quickly led to addiction. The abuse worsened.

"It's your job to take care of the kids," I can imagine Joseph saying after coming home drunk or high, or both. It caused problems because Mom just wanted help. She was trying to raise the baby on her own. "You're worthless," he'd tell her. "If it wasn't for me, you'd be nothing. I'm the man of the house."

On and on it went. He wore her down, mentally.

If she defended herself, he'd hit her. At first, it may not have been planned, or even something he did consciously. Over time, it became routine.

Even though she had a wild side to her, Mom knew where she wanted to go. She was a hard worker. Joseph was a slacker. Totally irresponsible. And it was the type of thing that she should have known about him before they were married. The time to learn that your husband is a party animal with no sense of responsibility and no desire to grow up is not after you walk down the aisle and have your first child. It appeared that Joseph didn't *want* to be a father. Mom had to play the hand she was dealt. But she didn't have to do it alone.

Choice Points:

- You own the choices you make - Whatever the outcome, good or bad, the natural consequences of your decisions are yours to own. That's good evidence to consider the consequences before you act.

- Look before you leap - Life is hard enough without self-imposed challenges. You reap what you sow. Make it easy on yourself by not jumping into situations, relationships, and impossible circumstances before you count the cost. The life you damage may not be just your own. There could be strings and ripples of consequences for generations to come.

- Play your cards well - No matter how unfair we think the hand we've been dealt is, we can't trade it in for a better hand. We don't get to choose our hand, but we do get to choose how we play the cards. Make the most of what you start with and seek to pass on a better hand to the next generation.

THE CHOICE IS YOURS: ASK FOR HELP

"Ask for help. Not because you are weak. But because you want to remain strong." — Les Brown

Mom gave birth to Joey in October 1978. Done and fed up with Joseph, she moved back to Santa Fe two months later.

Other than Joey, she had no family in Roswell. Grandpa was beginning to worry.

Black and blue from the beatings, and ashamed of it, she couldn't look anyone in the eye. But Grandpa could tell something was wrong. He had once spoken to his daughter daily, but, over time, daily turned to weekly. Sometimes, weeks would pass between calls.

Initially, Grandpa had called Mom every day to see if she needed anything, and to keep her focused. To guide her along the right track. When she figured out how to make it work on her own, he called less often. He was busy with his own set of responsibilities.

Still, Grandpa managed to convince her to return home where she could be close to family. Mom recalled for me one day the conversation she had with Grandpa.

"If you come home right now, Berta," he said, "we'll help you."

"I don't know."

Mom was still trying to prove she could make it. And she didn't want to impose on her parents because they were busy caring for her younger brother, my sick Uncle Gerard, who had cancer.

"Look, we'll figure it out," Grandpa said. "You come home. We will figure this out and help you get through this."

It took some time before Mom came around. She didn't want to admit she needed help, but she eventually saw the wisdom in throwing in the towel on my father and going back to Santa Fe where she could have the support of a family who loved her.

Mom said Grandpa told her, "Do not come home unless you're coming alone."

She did. But Joseph followed, and the abuse intensified.

As common as birth control was becoming, Mom still wasn't using protection. Thirteen months after Joey was born, Mom was pregnant again. It sounds ridiculous to me today, but I was an accident. And if one child was a handful, imagine how much more of a financial strain it was going to be with two young children. Joseph's and Mom's fighting continued to worsen.

Having me may have been one of the worst decisions Mom made. But if it hadn't happened, I wouldn't be here. *Roe v. Wade* passed in 1973, making first trimester abortions legal in the U.S. I don't think Mom ever considered it, but not many people would have blamed her if she had.

Her outlook was dismal. Nevertheless, I believe I was born for a reason. Maybe it was to test how strong Mom's independence really was.

During Mom's second pregnancy, Joseph did more than denigrate Mom, telling her how worthless she was. He also slapped her around. Punched her in the face. This man was completely out of control. I'm surprised she didn't lose the child. The abuse was that bad.

While she was mentally tough, Mom was also capable of showing great compassion. She tried to help Joseph change, but he was so hooked on heroin that he refused help. She tried to get him into rehab. He resisted. She even made appeals to his parents by saying things like, You can't bail him out of everything. It's not helping our marriage, and he's not going to learn.

But they enabled him.

Mom even used her network of friends to try to find Joseph jobs. He'd work for awhile, then he'd get fired because he'd show up to work high.

Despite Mom's best efforts to help him change, Joseph continued in his destructive lifestyle, unable and unwilling to seek help. Mom tried her best to make it work, but the stress became too much.

One night, Joseph came home high on heroin. By this time, he didn't need anything to set him off. Just being high was enough to get him on a "man rage." He walked in the door and immediately started throwing things. Whatever he could find. Pots and pans, lamps, books, tools, whatever was within reach. Then he punched Mom in the face.

She fell to the floor.

With bruises, a black eye, and a bloody nose, she crawled across the room and out the front door. She ran as fast as she could to the church next door. Joseph chased her. The church attendant opened the door and locked it behind them to shut Joseph out.

There were no smartphones in those days. Mom said she used the church's landline to call her cousin Ernie, a police officer in Santa Fe.

"Hello, Ernie?" she spoke through stifled tears. "He did it again. Can you come over?"

When she called Uncle Ernie, that was Joseph's clue to leave the house. He left in the same rage with which he had entered the house earlier. It wasn't long after that before Mom kicked him out of the house completely.

Choice Points:

- Sometimes, the best choice is still a bad choice - It was a bold move leaving my father with one child and another on the way. It was Mom's choice, and it was the best choice for her. She was determined to do whatever it took to raise her children to the best of her ability. And, truthfully, my father wasn't much help so she would have been raising two children on her own anyway, and dealing with the stress of the beatings and emotional anxiety that came with spousal abuse. The two years of hell she went through with my father meant she would have to endure a long-term recovery, and a huge change in her reality.

- There are times when you have to call for back up - Mom was the type of person who didn't like asking for help. Her pride, and independent spirit, drove her to prove that she was capable of handling whatever life tossed her way, and to do it on her own. But she did recognize that she could call Uncle

19

Ernie in her time of distress. Pride often gets in the way of asking for help. There's no shame in asking for help when you need it.

- Asking for help does not make you powerless - It is, in fact, a recognition of your own power to be able to seek help and be open to receiving it. Sharing your story with other survivors can be incredibly healing, as well.

THE CHOICE IS YOURS: BE AN OVERCOMER

"Although the world is full of suffering, it is also full of overcoming it." — Helen Keller

Being young, single, and recovering from abuse wasn't enough. Mom was blindsided when her baby girl was born with multiple health issues. Her doctor was given the unfortunate task of informing her she had given birth to a girl with a birth defect—a cleft pallet.

Mom had no clue what that meant. She asked a lot of questions. Her OB-GYN explained that I would need several surgeries to repair my pallet.

When I was old enough to understand, Mom told me her head was swimming with questions.

What exactly did that mean? What would be the implications for my long-term health? Would I be normal after the surgery? Could I have a normal childhood like every other little girl? Would the surgeries "fix" me completely?

All alone in her experience, she tried to understand it, but all this talk of cleft pallets and plastic surgery was a mystery to her. It was like a foreign language.

What it meant was, I would need to see a plastic surgeon, a nutritionist, a psychologist, and an ear, nose and throat doctor for several years. Overwhelming news. From Day One, I came into this world against insurmountable odds, with huge health issues, and several doctors monitoring me day and night.

If you don't know what a cleft pallet is, it means I was born without a roof in my mouth. That made eating very difficult. They brought in specialist after specialist to explain how she would have to care for me. I couldn't even feed on my mother's milk!

I couldn't have my first surgery until I was four months old. Meanwhile, Mom fed me with one of those rubber squeeze dropper syringes.

The only way I could get the sustenance I needed was to be spoon fed. If I wasn't fed with a spoon, I'd spit out whatever food passed my lips or it would come out through my nose. Even then, spoon feeding was a challenge. It didn't guarantee the food wouldn't escape through my nose, or come back out of my mouth once it went in.

I was in and out of hospitals until the age of seven. Plastic surgery was an ongoing thing, not a once-and-done type of thing. In other words, it took endurance.

It was a lot for Mom to handle. You would think things couldn't get worse..

But more bad news followed when meeting with the ear, nose and throat doctor. Several tests revealed that my hearing was not good. I was deaf in one ear and hard of hearing in the other. Literally.

Adding to the difficulties, my hearing problems meant I'd need tubes placed in my ears until age seven. To this day, we believe the abuse heaped upon my mother by Joseph was a significant contributor to my health issues. But Mom endured it to the end.

My grandparents told me on several occasions that she was tough, strong, and never complained. She was strong, independent, and carried a lot on those shoulders of hers. She handled the pressure. I might be biased, but I think she deserved the Mom of the Year Award.

I underwent twelve surgeries before second grade. Many of those surgeries took place during my kindergarten and first grade years. I was in and out of the hospital, with tubes in and out of my ears, undergoing plastic surgery to fix the roof of my mouth. I was out of school a lot. Behind on the normal learning that takes place in those critical formative years. I could barely read and couldn't hear anything. That meant I had to undergo speech therapy. Until I could talk, I learned to communicate with sign language, a useful skill I still use today.

Every year, from the first year until age seven, I'd see about seven different doctors, from nutritionists to speech therapists and plastic surgeons. Even psychiatrists, to help me cope with it all. That's how I spent my critical development years.

I was taken out of class for speech therapy or counseling once or twice a week. And other kids didn't understand. They would tease me, saying things like, "Why are you getting out of class so much?" or "Why are you always in special classes?"

But it didn't last long, because I was beginning to develop my hearing by kindergarten. I could speak with a lisp. Certain words were difficult to say, but I couldn't say some vowels correctly. Other kids would tease me for that.

Because I'd spent so long communicating with sign language, reading comprehension was tough. Eventually, with Mom's patient assistance, I'd get over that.

By the time I was seven years old, Joseph was out of our lives almost completely. He didn't want to be responsible for raising children to begin with. He surely didn't want to raise a sick one.

As soon as she could after moving back home to Santa Fe, Mom began looking for work. To support the family, she worked two jobs. From nine to five, she worked for the state of New Mexico as a mailroom clerk. At night and on weekends, she worked at McDonalds.

Until that time, Mom's living expenses had been minimal. Aunt Eva, Grandpa's sister, had a huge house in downtown Santa Fe and she offered Mom a place to stay until she could get back on her feet. We lived upstairs with a full kitchen, a bathroom, and two bedrooms—one for Mom and one for Joey and me. That allowed Mom to live rent-free. Grandpa provided the vehicle, also free. And Mom was on Medicaid, which took care of the medical expenses.

She was a hard worker too. It wasn't long after joining McDonalds that she was promoted to night shift manager. Being a night shift manager meant she worked longer hours. That meant more time away from Joey and me, but we knew she was doing the best she could. There were nights when Joey and I would sit in a McDonalds booth eating chicken nuggets and hot fudge sundaes while waiting for Mom's shift to end. This allowed the three of us to develop a strong bond. We didn't have money, but we had each other. That was enough for us.

While Mom did most of the raising, she had a great support system. My grandparents would often watch after us when Mom worked. I grew close to both grandparents, but they had their own challenges. Though my grandparents were busy with Uncle Gerard, who was in and out of the hospital for chemotherapy, they made it a point to make Joey and me feel special. They always welcomed us into their home with warm and open arms.

When she'd left Roswell and went back to Santa Fe, she hadn't wanted to ask her parents for help. She knew the handful my uncle was for them. But living with Aunt Eva was a big help.

That was actually one of the best decisions Mom ever made. Aunt Eva was like a second mother to Joey and me. She would cook for us, bathe us when Mom was exhausted from working all day, and do our laundry. Mom felt comfortable with Aunt Eva taking care of me with my health issues. There were times when she'd pick us up from preschool, or she'd iron Mom's clothes for her. She was a big help.

Aunt Eva worked for the state of New Mexico records department. She used her influence there to help Mom get her job. Networking works for government service too!

In New Mexico, getting a job with the state is the cat's meow. A lot of people covet those jobs because they're steady and provide opportunities for advancement.

Not long after getting on with the state, Mom got her first promotion—to microfilm technician. She moved up the ladder until she was manager of the tax examination department. Her determination, strong work ethic, and selflessness drove her to succeed.

Mom's divorce wasn't finalized yet as my father refused to sign the papers. I'm not sure why since he displayed no interest in raising his children. From that moment on, he was in and out of our lives, depending on his drug use.

It would be truer to say he was in and out of Joey's life. He didn't want anything to do with me. My health issues were too much for him to handle. Joey, being the first born, was something Joseph wouldn't let go of. That might have been the reason he wouldn't sign the divorce papers.

My father's parents had a similar attitude. They loved my brother, but they didn't want anything to do with me. Presumably, it was because of my health issues. As I grew older, I realized it wasn't worth trying to be a part of their lives.

Joey, however, kept a relationship with them. He'd get a call wishing him a happy birthday every year. Occasionally, he'd receive gifts.

I remember wondering if I did something to drive these people away. Why didn't they love me like they loved Joey? Eventually, I realized they didn't really want to be a part of Joey's life either. He was the first born, and that was something I think my father wanted to cling to, but they never supported us financially.

At the end of the day, Mom was a single mother working two jobs, living paycheck to paycheck, and supporting two children.

At one point, Joseph quit his job so he wouldn't have to pay child support. What kind of man does that? If he truly loved us, he wouldn't have quit his job to avoid paying child support, would he? These questions left me with a void in my heart.

To this day, I still question my father's motives. He owed hundreds of thousands of dollars in child support and never paid a penny of it. Mom was not the type of woman to let something like that go. She took him to court numerous times. She fought for child support until I was a senior in high school.

One time that really sticks out for me, Joseph couldn't get to Santa Fe so he, Mom, and the judge had a conference call. I overheard some of the conversation and was gobsmacked. The judge asked Joseph why he wasn't paying child support and he said, "I gave them (Joey and me) up years ago, so why should I pay child support?" It crushed me.

Even at that age, all I could do was wonder why this man who was supposed to be my father think he doesn't have to pay child support just because "he gave us up?" Unbelievable.

It was clear to me he didn't want us. Didn't love us.

Mom kept trying to get him to pay, while her friends tried to discourage her. I think she wanted Joey and me to see what kind of man he was. And we did.

25

Choice Points:

- Prepare yourself for setbacks - There's no way around it, setbacks are inevitable. Regardless of skill or talent, something will go wrong in your life. One time when setbacks are bound to happen is when trying your hand at something new or extremely challenging. No one succeeds by avoiding obstacles. Success is achieved by expecting setbacks and facing them head on.

- You can overcome any obstacle with faith - Faith is believing in yourself in the face of insurmountable obstacles. Mom endured struggles and committed herself to loving her children no matter what life threw at her. I learned that no matter how bad it is, no matter how dark it gets, you can overcome any obstacle with faith. Faith and my husband Shawn's encouragement are responsible for getting me where I am today. Faith is a necessity in overcoming life's challenges, so embrace it.

- Be an overcomer - For years, I fought anger welling up inside me because of my father's abuse of my mother. While it took years to get over it, I did eventually beat the demons. I had to allow myself to be vulnerable. It's not a sign of weakness, but strength. Talent will not help you overcome your fears, your challenges, or your self-limiting beliefs. Courage will. I know some of you are going through a dark place right now, but you'll be okay. Overcome the demons in your life. When you do, you'll be able to help others overcome theirs.

- Use your network - You have a network. It consists of your family and friends, and perhaps a few business associates. Don't be afraid to rely on your network to help you get where you want to be. No one is going to judge you for needing help. And if they do, they're not a part of your support network. Mom realized where to turn for help when she needed a place to live, a job, and help with her children. Your network could be critical in helping you overcome major obstacles in life. You can't do it all on your own.

THE CHOICE IS YOURS: NURTURE RELATIONSHIPS

"Everything worthwhile takes time, nurturing and love. When something isn't working, Love it more, nurture it more and give it time."
— Bryant McGill

The closest thing I had to a father, next to Grandpa, was Pete Deherrera, my stepfather. I called him Pops. He and Mom started dating when Mom and Joseph were on the divorce track. Aunt Eva introduced them to each other.

Like Mom and Aunt Eva, Pops worked for the state of New Mexico. It was a coveted job. Everyone wanted a job with the state. Pops worked in purchasing. One day, Mom said, Aunt Eva said to her, "I know a really good guy I think you should meet." The timing couldn't have been better. Joseph was on the way out and Mom wasn't the kind of woman to spend her life alone.

Right away, Pops took on the responsibility of raising Joey and me, including all of the challenges of dealing with a sick toddler. I was two years old and was in and out of hospitals like a piston in a race car. Pops would visit me in the hospital, bring me stuffed animals, and treat me like I was his own. He didn't miss a beat, just stepped right into it. My grandparents thought he was a saint.

By nature, he was caring and nurturing. Until he met Mom, he lived with his mother and took care of her. One of ten children, he understood how to compromise and get along well with others. Mom was his first wife, and his last. And when Mom came to the hospital to see me, he was there almost every single time. If Mom needed to run errands or go out for a bite to eat between work shifts, Pops would stay with me and keep me company. He made it a point to help out any way he could. By contrast, Joseph was inconsistent, showing up randomly and unexpectedly. Pops was steady and reliable.

He moved in with us in Tesuque a couple of years after he and Mom started dating. Three years later, they were walking down the aisle.

27

I didn't have a lot of friends in Tesuque. The ones I had were trailer park friends. You know, the neighborhood kids.

There were a couple of families in the trailer park we got a little close to. Joey and I went to school with the kids in those families, so it was convenient to hang out with them. And there were the Delgados. Genise and Gabriel were the children. Their parents were friends with Mom and Pops. We would go to their house and hang out once in a while. The parents would hang out and drink while Genise, Gabriel, and I would go outside and ride bikes together, or just run the neighborhood. That was my circle.

For me, friends mostly came and went. It was hard letting people into my life. In other words, I didn't spend much time nurturing friendships for fear of being hurt (Again, see Appendix 1 for tips on handling common fears.). Not having a father hardened me, and I just wasn't willing to open up.

Those trailer park friends are not in my life today. When I see them out and about, I'll say a friendly "hello," but I didn't spend enough time with them even then to get to know them very well. I certainly didn't have deep or intimate friendships with any of them. Not the kind of friendships that last a lifetime.

When I look back, I'm the girl without a childhood bestie. I'm the one without a high school yearbook inscription from her BFF. I was never anyone's bride's maid or maid of honor. I might have been well known by small town standards, but the number of childhood friends I had can be counted on one hand. You see, to have close friendships, you need to nurture them. You've got to spend time with people and get to know them. And I couldn't do that. I spent my time alone and wouldn't come out of that shell until well into high school.

Of course, I regret that. There were times when I was lonely. I believe that loneliness mostly stemmed from my father's abandonment. I didn't want to be hurt, or judged.

I was so concerned about being judged that I chose to sit back and observe. If I felt myself getting close to someone who could become a friend, I'd back away. To this day, I'm sure the few friends I did have had no clue this was going on inside of me. Not only was I protective of my heart, but I had such a hard shell around me that few people even noticed it.

When I'd visit my friends or acquaintances, they had fathers. Most of them had great relationships with their fathers. I envied that. I didn't know what that was like. I'd lie awake at night thinking, *What if my father was here? We could have family dinners, and play time. I could have what Emily has.* Eventually, I outgrew that. I'd get to the point where I thought, *Yeah, I don't need a father. I can do this on my own.*

Pops had adopted Joey and me. We had an intimate celebration that included some friends and family, including Grandma and Grandpa. Because of Pops, I experienced my second name change. Born an Ortega, Mom changed all of our names to Garcia, her maiden name. That happened after her divorce from Joseph was finalized. Then, Pops made us Deherreras. Shortly after that, he and Mom were in Vegas getting hitched.

While I had a difficult time letting people into my life, Pops made it easier. Mom worked two jobs, so Pops was the one who went on school field trips with me. And we bonded.

He also liked stream fishing for trout. He would take Joey and me fishing, and we loved it. If Mom was working—and she was always working—he'd make us dinner. He took us camping, traveling to different places, and acted as if he was our real father. In a sense, he was, and we loved him for it.

One weekend, he took Joey fishing while Mom was working. He told her, "When you get off work Saturday, why don't you and Joni join us?" And we did. Mom picked me up at Grandpa's house and we went camping, as a family.

When we arrived, I got out of the car and a stray dog bit me. Pops came unglued. He was not an angry man and didn't wear a sour face often, but this time he got upset because the dog's owner didn't have it on a leash. That's how protective he was over me.

Over time, I'd get over not having a father. I had Pops. Through the pain of my dysfunctional upbringing, he was one of the bright lights.

Choice Points:

29

- Nurture relationships - I've learned to put equity into relationships. What you put in is what you get out. That's true of personal relationships and business relationships. Pops taught me that if you don't let people in, people won't let you in. The long-term benefits of relationships include having a personal network lined up when you need one. Otherwise, building a business can be a long slog uphill.

- Don't dwell on the negatives - Life is full of struggles. Learn to see the bright lights. For me, that was Pops. Though my real father was absent much of the time, he filled the role for me in ways that Joseph couldn't. While I struggled to make friends, there were times during childhood when I had some and didn't value them. I've since learned to value every relationship I have.

- Define your family - Family isn't necessarily about whose blood flows through your veins. If you have a strong blood family, great! But if you don't, define who your family is. Stepparents, stepsiblings, half brothers and sisters, cousins, close friends ... whoever you are close to and have a connection with, make them your family. Take no relationship for granted.

THE CHOICE IS YOURS: DON'T LET THE PAST DEFINE YOUR FUTURE

"There are only two ways to approach life—as a victim or as a gallant fighter." — Merle Shain

When Mom gave Joseph an ultimatum to give up drugs or lose his family, he chose drugs. We'd see him occasionally, in short visits. But for the most part, he wasn't around much.

According to Mom, Joseph came home one evening high as a kite. That wasn't unusual. He was often out of control at that time of day. This particular evening, he threw things and punched her in the face. She went to the floor in tears. Instead of going for the phone to call Uncle Ernie as she would normally have done, she put her foot down.

Mom pulled herself up from the floor and that was it. She wasn't going to take the abuse anymore. When Joseph raised his fist to take another punch, Mom fought back. She pushed him back and scratched his face. Joseph, shocked, dropped his fist and sized her up good. It looked to her as if he saw something different in her eyes. At the very least, he'd have noticed the tears were gone and replaced with a fiery confidence. She squared her shoulders, pointed her finger at him, and ordered him out of the house.

That's when she gave him her final ultimatum, she said. "You get rid of the drugs. Choose them or your family. You can't have both."

She told me later that he looked like he didn't take her seriously and was about to speak when she cut him off.

"No!" Mom shook her head and stomped her foot, wagging her finger. "I mean it. I'm done. Lose the drugs or you're out."

Joseph uttered some expletive and exited the door. Mom didn't know where he went that night, and didn't care. He was gone. He wasn't punching her. That's all she cared about. But she knew he'd be back, and wasn't likely to give up the drugs. He may have even gone to get more, for all she knew. When he returned, she thought, he was still going to be angry. Probably ready to hit her again.

31

She went through his dresser drawers, the bathroom, the living room, the tool-shed, and every corner of the house to find anything that belonged to him. She shoved it into garbage bags, and dragged them to the street. Next, she picked up the phone, called Greyhound, and ordered a bus ticket for Roswell. Finally, she took the car, drove down to the bus station, picked up the ticket, and came back home. Patiently, she waited for Joseph to return.

When he did return, hours later, Mom ran to the door. She could see he was still high and still angry. She threw the bus ticket in his face and told him she wanted him out that night. She threw the bus ticket at him and told him she never wanted to see him again.

Joseph looked at the bus ticket lying on the floor. He picked it up. Without a word, he turned and walked out.

I was about a year-and-half when that happened.

While Mom cut Joseph off, she didn't cut off his parents. She let them have periodic visits. The relationship she had with them wasn't perfect, but it was decent. And my godmother, Joseph's sister, also had a pretty good relationship with Mom. She wasn't about to cut off the whole family just because my father loved drugs more than his own children.

Whenever they had the time, they would drive from Roswell to Santa Fe and pick Joey and me up from Grandma's and Grandpa's house. Of course, they'd bring Joseph. That didn't thrill Mom, but she lived with it. They would take us to the mall, to an ice cream shop in downtown Santa Fe, or to Woolworth's where we could eat Frito pies. Then we'd go back to their hotel and play games or hang out. This went on for about three years.

So we got to see our father during those times, but he wasn't in our lives other than for those interactions, and only when his parents were around.

With medical issues, doctor visits, scheduled surgeries, all I needed was the lack of a father figure in my life to make me see that I was not like other children my age. On top of that, they held me back in first grade, so I had to do it twice. That put me at a further disadvantage, but it was just one more thing.

One day—I was about six years old and Joey was seven—Joseph and his mom were arguing. He took Joey and me, left his parents there at the hotel in Santa Fe, and drove to Roswell. He went into the house where he was living with his parents, packed a bagful of clothes—for himself, because he didn't have any clothes for Joey and me—and the three of us started walking.

He was taking us to Wyoming, hitchhiking. When Mom found out, she freaked. Joseph's parents had no clue where we were. Mom contacted Joseph's brother, who went looking for us.

Joey and I thought we were on some wild adventure with our father. We didn't know any better. But Mom drove to Roswell looking for us. When she found us, she let Joseph have it. That was it for the weekend visits with Joseph.

She later told us she had crazy things going through her head. Things like, *What if they get in a car accident?* And when she found out we were walking the streets of Roswell, she wondered about some random trucker picking us up, or some old man in a white van, and selling us into child slavery.

As it turned out, he'd had his license revoked and shouldn't even have been driving. The vehicle was his parents' too, so he left them stranded back in Santa Fe.

When I was old enough to understand the concept, I knew that Joseph was dysfunctional. I chose not to have anything to do with him any more. In my mind, if he didn't love Joey and me enough to quit his drug habit, then I wasn't going to be around him. It was that simple.

Until then, I couldn't comprehend it. I was a young child without a father. It never crossed my mind why that was the case. My friends had fathers. While I felt a lack in my soul over the absence of a father figure, I didn't feel the effects of it emotionally until I was old enough to understand the concept of fatherly love.

I thought it was my fault. I beat myself up wondering why my father chose his drug problem over me. What could I have done?

One night, a friend invited me to her house for dinner. I showed up and we played, then her mom called us to the table. We sat around a big table, ate some home cooking, and talked. I noted that she had a father, and he was a nice guy. He talked to his wife and children respectfully, valued their opinions, and seemed to enjoy their company. Why didn't I have that? I started to feel resentful, bitter, angry.

By the time I was eight years old, there was so much anger built up inside of me. I couldn't wrap my head around why a parent could leave his children. He never sent me birthday cards or called to see how I was doing. He didn't pay child support. He took no interest in his family whatsoever. What kind of person could be that way? I wondered.

There were times when I'd cry myself to sleep. I'd shut my bedroom door, curl up in my blankets, and let the tears fall until I drifted away. I'd fall asleep wishing my life could be at least somewhat close to normal.

For most of my childhood, I wondered when my father would get his next hit. I made a commitment to myself that I'd figure life out on my own—just like Mom had. There were times when I felt alone. There were other times when I didn't feel worthy. Why did all of these things happen to me? Why did God, if there was one, put me on this earth?

I questioned a lot of things, including my own existence. What was the point?

It was a lot for a young girl to bear. My father's addiction meant he couldn't function most days, even if he tried. It's sad to say, but taking another hit of heroin was his way of facing life's battles. If he didn't get his hits when he needed them, he would go through the painful experience of withdrawal.

His mom called it a sickness. She got him into rehab one time, but he didn't make it. As soon as he went into withdrawal, she could see the pain he was going through and that was it. She got him out.

When Mom would bring it up, Joseph's mom would tell her he can't do it; when he stops using, he goes through withdrawal and gets sick, she said. So, in essence, they cared more about his comfort than his life. It was almost like it was okay to be an addict.

Mom tried for a while, but gave up after Joseph and his parents put up a wall of resistance. Who could blame her? He had abused her, and she had spent a couple of years enduring that while trying to be his sole support, which only made her bitter toward him.

In the end, she wanted nothing to do with him. She was all that Joey and I had, so we did whatever Mom wanted us to do. If she told us not to speak to him, we didn't. If she didn't want us speaking to his parents, we didn't. And that's exactly what happened. She cut us off from that side of the family, except for birthdays and special occasions. Even then, they only talked with me one time.

I must have been eleven or twelve. They had called for Joey. After speaking to him, they asked for me. It was strange because Mom had been having issues with Joey. He was expelled from one of the Catholic schools in Santa Fe. He was getting into trouble and Mom was struggling. After discussing that with Joseph's mom and dad, they asked to talk with me.

I was suspicious, but got on the phone.

When I did, Joseph's dad lectured me. Just like that. It went something like this:

"I can't believe you won't let your father into your life. You should respect him. He's your father. If you keep this up, you'll regret it because you didn't spend time with him. If he dies, it will weigh on your conscience."

That ticked me off.

"You know what?" I said. "Number one, you guys left me. If you wanted a relationship with me, you should have come to me for that. I shouldn't have to hunt you down to have a relationship with my father."

Then he started talking to me about how much trouble Mom was having with Joey and blaming her because Joey was in trouble at school.

"You know," I laid into him. "You have never done anything to support us, or to help us. You haven't paid a dime, not a penny have you contributed to my clothes, food for us, or to help pay some rent, so I don't think you have a right to say any of that."

Mom was working two jobs at the time to support us, and these critics weren't contributing anything. I noticed. "Not once have you

35

asked, 'Can we help you with this, or help you with that?' And then you want to come and say all of that me? I don't think so." I took a deep breath. "I don't want anything more to do with you or my father." And hung up the phone.

I was done.

Angry and bitter about the situation, I wouldn't allow them to blame Mom and me for the decisions they had made.

That night, I cried myself to sleep again. I hid it well. Nobody knew I was shedding tears. Not even Mom. She had no clue. I guess I was a lot like her in that regard.

Choice Points:

- Believe in yourself - We've all had days when we question whether we have the strength to continue. The first step is to believe that you can, and that you will. Looking backwards will not move you forward. It is okay to let go of the past.

- Get rid of the toxic people in your life - Toxic people will drag you down. Joseph was toxic. His drugs and abuse of Mom was just heavy weight in our lives. Mom did the right thing when she kicked him to the curb.

- Make hard choices even if they're painful - Some of the most painful experiences are making hard choices. Nevertheless, they've got to be made. I'd have liked to have had a relationship with my father and his family, but when they blamed Mom and me for their choices, that couldn't happen. Your success in life is determined in part by how much you're willing to put up with from others.

- Attitude makes all the difference - Give yourself a chance to heal from old wounds. Let them shape you in positive ways rather than negative. Allow light into your life through people who love you, self-help books, exercise or meditation, positive self talk, faith, focus, and believing in yourself.

- Deal with your past - We all have a past, a present, and a future. How you choose to deal with your past in the present will define your future.

THE CHOICE IS YOURS: BE AMBITIOUS

"I love to see a young girl go out and grab the lapels. Life's a bitch. You've got to go out and kick ass." - Maya Angelou

I avoided relationships by keeping myself busy. At thirteen, I was as agenda-driven as a 21st-century corporate executive. My desire was to help support my family. It became a personal obsession.

I knew I was destined to be my own boss one day. Make my own money. Manage employees. I said that to Grandma once. She believed me, telling me I'd rule the world.

I'd role play business scenarios, dressing up in Grandma's high heels, a long skirt, slide Grandma's glasses up my nose, and act like I was Meg Whitman or Carly Fiorina (Appendix 2 showcases some of my top influences). I'd play the executive and Grandpa was my employee. I'd tell him what to do, and he'd laugh, asking me where I'd come up with these things.

It was a different world than what a mailman was accustomed to, for sure. But that was the world I dreamed of.

Grandpa and I would sit together, watching Judge Judy. I'd watch her mannerisms and the way she spoke to people in her courtroom. I'd think, *I can be that lady.* I saw myself as a future director or executive.

I must have been eleven or twelve years old when I realized that if I wanted nice things, or if I wanted anything at all, I was going to have to work for them. My mother barely made ends meet, and that meant there wasn't anything left over after the bare necessities.

She had saved up enough money to move us out of Aunt Eva's house and was lucky enough to find a true, classic gentleman who knew my grandfather. Like Grandpa, he was a mailman. He was the sweetest old man. He managed a trailer park in Tesuque, New Mexico and would occasionally have some trailers up for sale. Grandpa asked him one day if he had one he could sell to Mom. He sold one he'd repossessed to Mom with owner-financing.

We lived in that three-bedroom trailer in Tesuque for much of my childhood after that. It was Mom's greatest achievement at the time. Finally, we had a place of our own to call home.

Since I could see Mom working hard to pay off the trailer and put food on the table, I didn't ask for a lot of things. Instead, seeing her work so hard to put a stable roof over our heads, I developed a desire for my own possessions, things I could buy with my own hard-earned money. That desire grew along with my age.

Because I could see what Mom was going through to raise Joey and me, I've looked at life through a different lens than most people do. I wanted to help. Mom thought it was cute, but I was serious. I really wanted to help. If I could work a job, make money to buy the clothes I wanted, and have some left over to help her pay the bills, that would be incredible. I was an ambitious thirteen year old.

Joey was into designer clothes. He always had the hippest clothes, the latest trendy attire, and I wanted to be like him. So if he was wearing Guess, I wanted to wear Guess. If he was sporting Girbauds, I wanted Girbauds. And that meant I needed a job.

I wanted a job. And I was ready for one at thirteen.

Grandpa went through the trouble of finding out what the legal age was for obtaining a work permit. Fifteen, he said. When I found out I wasn't old enough to work, I was devastated. If someone wants to work, what difference does it make how old they are? That was my way of thinking. After that, I counted the days until I turned fifteen.

Choice Points:

- Be patient - All good things have their time. I was ready to work at thirteen, but the world wasn't ready for me then. I was not mature enough. I'd have to wait two years before getting my first job, but the desire for that job built within me, preparing me for the occasion. It's a mystery how that works, but it does. Just because you want something today doesn't mean you should have it today. Learn to wait for the good things. You'll enjoy and respect them more when they come along.

- Create an environment for ambition to take root - Surround yourself with positive people who support you and have their own ambitions. A lot of women don't have people like this in their lives. Growing up, I didn't know anyone interested in self development. As I grew older, however, I met some people interested in reading self-help books and who didn't think it was weird to improve their finances, health, or relationships. Finding like-minded people changed everything.

THE CHOICE IS YOURS: BE WHO YOU ARE

"Life is a matter of choices, and every choice you make makes you." — John C. Maxwell

While Joey and I lived with Mom in Tesuque for most of our childhood, there were times when we lived with Grandpa and Grandma in Santa Fe. When we didn't live with them, we spent an awful lot of time at their house. It worked for us because Mom held down two jobs, and other logistical challenges made it convenient.

I carried a lot of anger on my shoulders. As a teenager, I finally opened up to Grandpa. He was willing to listen. He became the only person I could trust, the one I could count on for everything, the father figure I didn't have. Grandpa encouraged me every step of the way.

Despite this support, I felt no sense of purpose. I wasn't happy. I needed a clear path in life. Grandpa opened the door.

He could tell if something wasn't right. If I had a bad day at school, or something happened that set me off. If I wasn't hanging out with anybody that day and feeling lonely, if I wasn't feeling worthy of love, or if I was embroiled in some teenage existential crisis, Grandpa could see it in my face. He'd say something like, "Joni, I can see something's wrong. Let's talk about it."

He might have had to pull a few times on the rope, a sort of emotional tug-of-war game, but he could open me up. He was the only one who could.

When he got me to talking and hearing what was bothering me, he'd say—and he said this frequently—"*Mija*, you need God in your life." *Mija* is Spanish for "my daughter." Grandpa would use it as a term of endearment when he was being fatherly. Otherwise, he called me "Shorty."

There were times when he and I would sit on his patio in Santa Fe and talk for hours. He'd listen to whatever was ailing me. We'd walk out on the patio, I'd take a seat in his chair, and he'd say, "That's my chair, Shorty." I'd jump over to the other chair and we'd pray together.

41

"Lord," he'd pray, something like this: "Give Joni the strength to overcome her struggles, give her insight and wisdom to know how to deal with the people who trouble her, and help her to understand her purpose here on earth. I know you have a purpose for her. Help her to find it."

It took me a while to believe in Grandpa's God. If I couldn't trust the people I could see, how was I ever going to trust some God I couldn't? I had trouble believing in God, in purpose, in myself. I continued to question things, maybe even more after that. If there was a God, I wondered, why would he allow my family to go through what we went through? Grandpa's prayers, while sweet, didn't do anything to dispel the anger. I couldn't let it go.

I didn't let him know that. I had my devil-may-care attitude, after all.

Despite my attitude, my grandparents had rules, and I respected them. One was mandatory church attendance. Another was Catholic catechism classes. I honored those wishes, and was an altar girl too. They told me if I was going to stay with them, then that was something I was going to have to do.

Joey tried following the rules, to an extent, but it was more difficult for him. When he was old enough, about fifteen, he quit attending Mass and serving at church. Grandma and grandpa were older by then and kicked him out.

"I can't take care of you and your sister if you're not going to listen," Grandpa told him. "You can't stay here any more with that attitude."

So Joey left. He went back to living with Mom where he could have more freedom.

Grandpa wanted to ensure I didn't turn out like Joey, and my father. "You don't have to be like them," he said to me on more than one occasion. "The only person you can change is yourself."

And I took it to heart, too. In spite of the doubts, the questioning, and the anger. Eventually, it would lead me to engage in personal soul searching. In the meantime, I went through that "poor me" phase, feeling sorry for myself. Joey, on the other hand, got stuck in it.

I feared becoming a drug addict, like Joey and my father. At this particular time in my life, that fear was strong. The self-talk was the worst it's ever been in my life. The demons wouldn't stop talking. *No one is going to love you,* they'd say. *You're going to end up just like Joey,* or *You're going to walk the same path as your father.*

I didn't try drugs. I was too much of a chicken. But the temptation was there, and Mom made sure I'd see what drugs did to Joey.

"You see that?" she'd say on repeat. "You want to end up like that?"

Joey would sniff paint, get high, and start acting weird. He was buzzed out of his mind. Mom tried to steer him straight, but he just wouldn't go. Then she'd give up and let him ride the high.

The way I carried myself publicly back then was very different than the cry-myself-to-sleep me. I was popular in school, largely because of my devil-may-care attitude. I didn't fear anything. Or so people who knew me thought. The tough exterior I put on made some people reluctant to approach me. Maybe they could sense the anger, the frustration. I didn't care. I was a girl with a chip on my shoulder.

It made it hard to make friends. People couldn't relate to me. As a result, I didn't have close friends. I didn't trust anyone enough to allow them into my circle. If they got close, made a real effort, I'd be okay for a while, then I'd put distance between us. I'd get to feeling lonely.

It was this fear of rejection that drove me, a fear of getting hurt. I had this anger, and questioned my existence. My purpose.

As far as I knew, I didn't have a purpose. I started dressing differently. I began wearing short shorts and short tops, mostly to get attention. I'd sneak out of the house to be with boys. If my grandparents caught me dressed that way, they'd make me change clothes. But I'd throw the short shorts and tank tops in a backpack and leave the house, changing later when I had a chance. I didn't want them to see that girl.

Of course, the boys I'd attract dressed like that weren't the kind of boys my grandparents would approve of either. They were more like

Joey. The bad boy type. Boys like Joseph. The kind of boys Mom liked when she was younger.

There was a part of me who wanted to be one of the cool kids. I wanted to hang out with them because I thought they were going to protect me. Even though I knew they were up to no good, I wanted to impress them. In the back of my head, I was afraid of becoming like them, and I sought their approval. This double-mindedness kept me on the edge of sanity, but barely.

An incident in the seventh grade illustrates this double-mindedness—the fear of turning out like Joey coupled with the bullheadedness of my pre-teen chip on the shoulder.

Joey invited me to go for ice cream one evening in his gray Dodge Neon. As we climbed into the vehicle, he announced we'd be making a quick stop at a friend's house to pick something up. I had a gut feeling he was up to no good.

Sure enough, on our way to Baskin Robbins, he pulled into a driveway about five blocks from our house. It was pitch dark and there was a long row of cars up and down the street. Joey parked in front of the driveway like he owned the place. He told me to stay in the car because he would only be a few minutes.

While sitting there, my heart pounded. Hard. Parked in front of the driveway where everyone could see me as they walked into the party, I got anxious. A few minutes felt like hours, so I got out of the car and went inside.

Joey saw me. He told me to stay in the living room while he walked to the back room. Random men and women were sprawled out in the living room, drunk, practically naked, and barely functioning. My heart raced even faster. My head was spinning. I couldn't decide whether to get the heck out of there and walk home or wait for Joey to return from the back room.

It was December, so there was a Christmas tree in the house. I hid behind it. I didn't want anyone recognizing me or knowing I was there, so I ducked behind the fir tree decorated with beer bottles, bongs, and pot pipes.

You know when you have a bad feeling about a situation? How it rises up from the gut and sticks in your throat?

I could feel the tension building up inside. How was I going to get home? I thought, for a moment, of running to the back room, grabbing my brother, and getting out of there. I was afraid someone in the back room would start a fight with Joey, or the cops would show up and everyone, including me, would go to jail.

At thirteen, I knew what was going on in the back room. Joey was making a drug deal. All I could think of at that moment was to pray to Grandpa's God that we'd get out of there safely.

Sitting behind the tree waiting for Joey, I wondered if my life was in danger. I put on my poker face. The best one I had at the time, anyway. I couldn't be seen as some frightened little girl. So I remained calm and worked my way to the front door, slowly. Nobody seemed to realize I was leaving, they were so far gone. When I got outside, I ran to the car and waited for Joey to come out.

I promised myself, "I'll give him five more minutes. If he doesn't show up, I'll walk home."

Right on time, Joey came out of the house, mad as ever. He had run through the house looking for me and couldn't find me. Why was he mad at me? *He* had put *me* in danger. I should be mad at him, I thought.

I didn't speak to him all the way home. When we reached the driveway, I asked Joey, "What were you thinking to go there and bring me along? You know we could have been killed?"

It was as if he didn't know what had just happened was wrong. He begged me not to tell Mom where we went. Of course, I was a loyal sister and held that secret tight to my chest all the way through school. In hindsight, I wonder if I should have.

Joey was everything to me. He was my best friend, and I was not going to throw him under the bus. I kept my mouth shut. We never got the ice cream he promised me.

At the time, I dated a boy who was obsessive over me. He wouldn't let me talk to other guys or have other friends. If he saw me talking to someone else, he'd get upset and make a scene. He wanted me all to himself. I latched onto that because I wasn't getting affection anywhere else. Mom wasn't affectionate. I had no father to model how a man should treat a woman. Pops and Grandpa were the only two examples I had, and I wasn't paying close enough attention to let it sink in.

Marty and I dated for over a year before I finally got tired of it. One day, when we were in eighth grade I said, "You know what? I've had enough of this. Why don't you take a hike?"

Marty got mad.

We were standing at my locker and he slammed the door. Hard. It bounced and hit me in the face. Right away, it swelled up and I had a black eye. I went to the nurse and she sent me home from school early.

When Mom saw me, she asked what happened.

"Oh, nothing," I lied. I told her some kids were messing around and I got hit with a locker.

Joey, of course, knew every kid in town. He was out and about that afternoon, hanging out at Walmart, and ran into one of his friends, a boy who went to school with me. His friend asked if he had heard what happened to me.

Joey hadn't heard so his friend told him Marty got pissed off at me breaking up with him and hit me.

Joey came unglued. When he got home, he questioned me about my black eye.

"I got hit by a locker," I said. "It was an accident."

"Why don't you tell Mom what really happened?"

After some back and forth, I finally came clean and told the truth. Mom took me to the principal's office the next day and filed a police report. Marty ended up getting arrested over it.

After that, I thought more about what kind of life I wanted to have. Did I really want to date guys like that? Did I want to go through the same turmoil my mom went through?

Mom was terrified because she had gone through all of that with Joseph. She didn't want me to go through it, too. She kept a closer eye on me.

Fear can crush a person, mentally. It can shut down your brain and hold you back. After the Marty incident, I became more self-aware.

I'm not going to let fear control my life, I promised myself. With that, I decided to change my mindset.

Choice Points:

- Respect authority - As an entrepreneur, you're an authority of your own. If you want people to respect your authority, then you've got to model that behavior by respecting the authority of others. Despite the strictness of Grandpa's and Grandma's rules, I respected and obeyed them. Joey could not. I believe this made a big difference in both of our lives.

- Choose your associates carefully - Jim Rohn said, "You are the average of the five people you spend the most time with." Another famous saying is "Bad company corrupts good character." Who you associate with is a reflection of who you are.

- If your direction is off, change your mindset - Everything you do is a reflection of your mindset. The clothes you wear, the friends you have, the decisions you make. It all comes from your mindset. When you change your mindset, you change who you are from the inside out, and it will reflect in everything you do.

THE CHOICE IS YOURS: STAND UP FOR YOURSELF

"You either walk inside your story and own it, or you stand outside your story and hustle for your worthiness" — Brené Brown

The Marty incident was my wake-up call. After that, Mom transferred me to St. Michael's.

I didn't want to go to a Catholic school. I begged Mom not to do it. I wanted to be in public school with my friends. Nevertheless, the next year, in ninth grade, I was enrolled.

And that was that.

One of the first things I did was try out for the softball team. Sports allowed me to channel some of the anger I carried. Most of the family didn't get that involved in my sports. Grandpa was the only one who ever came to watch me play. Mom and Pops were focused on Joey's athletic achievements, praising him for his skills. But she was not that way with me. It pushed me to beg for attention.

I was confident, even as a freshman, that I would at least make the junior varsity team. If I made varsity, that would icing on the cake.

Trying out for the varsity team, I stood against some strong, intimidating girls. Even though I was wowed by these juniors and seniors, I stood tall and confident, proud. I simply acted like I knew what I was doing.

These girls tormented me. They would call me names and gang up on me in the hallways. Two of them were sisters, and one had a crush on Joey, who was not interested. So, the "Spurned One" decided she didn't like him. he other sister was the catcher of the St. Michael softball team, and her best friend was the pitcher. They were huge girls, all seniors.

The first week of school, I tried out for the team and made the cut. The Spurned One taunted me, saying things like, She can't be on the team. She's a freshman.

One day, while walking down the hall, minding my own business, the pitcher intentionally bumped shoulders with me as she strolled by. I thought, *What's with this girl?*

The next day, I was walking through the hallway and she took a piece of gum out of her mouth. Then she threw it at me with my back turned. I had gum goo stuck in my hair for the rest of the day.

In the lunch room later that day, she called me names, bullying me.

"What is your issue?" I asked. The cocky devil-may-care attitude reared its head. I should have been scared. This girl towered over me. But I was shocked at her behavior.

She put her fist up like she was going to punch me. Six feet tall, twice my size in body weight, this monster of a girl threatened to kick my butt because she thought a freshman wasn't ready for the softball team.

I had been through the lunch line and was holding a bowl of salad in my hands. I weighed my options. I could punch her, run, or throw salad in her face. I didn't want to get suspended on the first week of school, so I threw my lunch in her face. Was it the right thing to do? At the time, it seemed like it.

Covered in Ranch dressing, she grew red-faced angry. I could tell she wanted to beat me to a pulp.

Luckily for me, Joey was sitting at a table across the lunch room. He glanced over to see what was going on and saw this bigger girl about to make hamburger meat out of me. He jumped over five tables to come to my rescue.

I'm not exaggerating to call this girl a monster. Joey stood six feet tall and weighed nearly two hundred pounds. She towered over him.

Joey was popular in school, but his classmates didn't know he had a sister. Until that day. I wondered if he was embarrassed to say he had a sister. But when he jumped the tables in the lunch room, lunging to my defense, everyone found out who I was.

The girl's boyfriend stood beside her. He was a big football jock. When Joey got involved, he got involved. And he was bigger than

Joey. Once the fight broke up, we all ended up in the principal's office.

I thought, *Oh, boy. Mom is not going to be a happy camper when she finds out both of her children went to the principal's office for fighting.* I thought we'd be suspended or expelled.

Joey had been involved in other incidents before, so it could have happened that way. We both explained what happened to the school disciplinarian, but he wasn't buying it. He was a retired Santa Fe police officer, and I think he already had his mind made up about the Deherreras, Joey and Joni.

Joey and I were total opposites. I'd never been in trouble in school while Joey was constantly in some kind of trouble. The retired officer suspended Joey immediately. Then he began to talk about suspending me.

I felt like screaming, but I stayed calm.

"My brother was trying to protect me," I said. "If you want to suspend someone, you should suspend the six-foot monster who attacked me for no reason."

That got his attention. He brought the other girl in with her six-foot boyfriend, also a senior. The girl admitted what happened and apologized. I'm not sure why, but she knew she was wrong. The disciplinarian sent the two of them home for the day. Because it wasn't the first time Joey had been in trouble, they warned him that other incidents would lead to his being expelled from school.

I felt awful. The first time Joey tried doing the right thing, he got in trouble for it. And he was protecting *me*.

I thought it was wrong that he got in trouble. I felt like it was my fault and beat myself up over it. Had I not thrown salad in that girl's face, we wouldn't have been in that situation. I learned from that experience to examine my choices in order to influence future outcomes.

Things changed for me after that. Nobody wanted to mess with me any more.

I think I let that girl get to me because I felt I needed to be strong. There was no one at home I could talk to. I had a choice to make. I could quit softball and let these girls win, or persist through the awful situation into personal victory.

At that moment, I hated school. It was the first time in my life I felt that way. I didn't like going somewhere I wasn't accepted.

Most of my friends attended public school. Mom sent me to a Catholic private school away from them all. Since I had difficulty making friends to begin with, I needed something to help me feel like I belonged there. Trying out for the varsity softball team was the one thing that excited me.

I didn't expect to make it. But I knew I had to try.

Choice Points:

- Confidence and persistence are more important than talent - I would not be where I am today if I didn't have the courage to try out the varsity softball team as a freshman in high school. Sports gave me a sense of purpose and taught me a lot about myself. Many of us want to quit when things get tough. We lose self-confidence and forget our purpose. Talent is no substitute for confidence and persistence in the face of obstacles.

- Never surrender - There can be ugly people in the world. Instead of getting angry or intimidated, stand up for yourself. If I had let those varsity softball girls break me down, that would have been surrendering to the demons. It would have been like quitting, and that's what they wanted. They were jealous. No matter how hard life gets, keep pushing toward your goals. Quitting isn't an option.

- Be mentally tough - One of the hardest things I've had to do was learn to work as a team with those girls in high school who wanted to beat me down. That environment forced me to be mentally tough. There will always be obstacles you can't control.
  Accept that and feed yourself a different narrative. *I'm confident, worthy, strong, smart, and talented.* Say it over and over again until you believe it.

- Be solutions-oriented - Had I been more solutions-oriented in the ninth grade, the confrontation I had with the senior varsity players on my softball team might not have turned out so ugly. Today, situations like that don't turn sour because I'm a solutions-oriented manager. If I have an issue with someone, I'll go to them and say, "Let's sit down and talk about this." Think on your feet and work to mitigate conflict rather than escalate it.

- Face your demons, sooner rather than later - My success has a lot to do with me overcoming the difficulties of my childhood, fighting my demons, and winning. No matter what your past has been like, it is not your destiny. Overcoming the pain of my past has helped me become a better spouse, mother, and leader. Sports helped me develop the skills to do that. It doesn't have to be sports for you. Find something that challenges you and builds your character, something that helps you develop the skills that lead to achievement and an overcoming mindset. Facing your demons head on helps you become a better and more humble person. The sooner the better.

THE CHOICE IS YOURS: BE PERSISTENT

"Obstacles don't have to stop you. If you run into a wall, don't turn around and give up. Figure out how to climb it, go through it or work around it." — Michael Jordan

At fourteen, almost one year to the day before turning fifteen, I started researching companies within driving distance from Tesuque to see who might hire a teenager with a worker's permit. Not many companies wanted to take a chance on a fifteen-year-old girl. Fast food restaurants would. And it didn't matter to me. I was so eager to work, I'd have taken any job that came along. I'd have shoveled cow manure if it earned me enough income to help Mom pay some bills, and if I could buy my own Guess jeans.

Mom wasn't a big fan of me working at fifteen. She had a lot on her plate and didn't want to drive me to and from work. When I asked her to drive me to get my work permit, there was always some reason she didn't have the time. Granted, she had some pretty good excuses. After all, she did have a lot going on. In fact, she had so much she could barely keep her head screwed on straight.

For starters, she was working two jobs. That alone was enough to keep her busy. Plus, she was busy taking Joey to and from his sporting events—games and practices.

When I asked Mom to drive me to get my work permit, she didn't agree. She asked questions. "What are you going to spend the money on? How am I going to find the time to do that?"

And then she told me I'd probably end up spending all the money on junk things.

I realized she was looking for a way out, so I contemplated who else could take me to get my permit.

Mom really didn't have the time. She would be up in the morning by six, drop Joey and I off at Grandma's house in Santa Fe, about a half hour drive from Tesuque, have breakfast with us, and head to work. She worked at the state from 8:00 a.m. until 5:30 p.m., then she had to be at McDonald's at 6:30 p.m. She'd work there until midnight and pick Joey and I up from Grandma's house—unless we were already with her—and take us home. There really was no time for taking me for a work permit.

Fortunately, when I turned fifteen, Uncle Gerard's health had stabilized enough that my grandparents could step up their involvement in the lives of Joey and me. They liked watching us too, and we spent about half our time there. I did, anyway. Joey spent a little less time there because he would often stay at home by himself. I thought that if I could win Grandpa over, then I could convince him to take me to get my worker's permit.

Rather than ask directly, I approached it a little more slyly. I probed him with leading questions. "Grandpa, how old were you when you had your first job?"

Like a lot of Grandpas, he was a great storyteller. He told me how he'd go door to door selling milk at fifteen. That impressed me. Then Grandma told me the story about her first job working as a waitress at some fancy restaurant in Santa Fe. That didn't turn out so well as she was fired on the second day for messing up customer orders.

Wow, I thought, *Grandma and Grandpa are super-excited about telling me how they got into the workforce.*

That led me to asking what they thought about me getting a job. The response was immediate. In unison, they agreed.

I think they saw it as an opportunity for me to take on responsibility and learn how the real world works. For one thing, it would get me out of the house and allow me to do some things for myself.

From time to time, Grandpa would say things like, "I'm not going to be here forever, so you need to grow up and do things on your own. You shouldn't ask permission or wait for someone to guide you."

He knew how to give me things to think about.

When I found out Grandpa and Grandma were fully supportive, I told Grandpa that I had a list of companies who would hire me if I had a worker's permit. He said something encouraging along the lines of, "Shorty, I think that is a really good idea. Your mother works so hard, and I think she would appreciate you making some extra money."

I didn't tell him I'd already spoken to Mom and she wasn't on the same page.

Grandpa and I were on the same page. I asked, "Grandpa, when can you take me to get my permit?"

"Shorty, if your mother is okay with it, I'll take you."

Hmmm, I thought. *How am I going to get around to telling Mom?*

I already knew how she felt about the situation. If she expressed her sentiments to Grandpa, then I was guaranteed not to have a job. I felt I had no choice but to lie. I hated that, but I thought it would be the only way I could get a job. I told Grandpa I had already talked to her and "as long as you can take me, she's all for it." There may have been a twinkle in my eye.

He fell for it. Looking back, I think he really trusted me. He must have assumed I wouldn't lie to him. It ate me up inside that I had to lie to my grandfather, but it may have been the only way I could get a job. And I wanted one more than I wanted anything else.

"Okay, Shorty, we'll get your permit to work," he promised.

The day after my fifteenth birthday, Grandpa drove me to get my worker's permit. In fact, that was his gift for me that year. As soon as I had the permit in hand, I began my job search.

At the state department, they were hiring teenagers to work the mailroom, but they weren't hiring permit workers. That was a little disappointing because Mom probably could have gotten me in. I decided not to broach that subject with her and filled out applications in the neighborhood instead.

I completed about ten applications. After a few days, the manager at Taco Bell called me for an interview. Grandpa was happy to drive me to it.

On the day of my interview, I was nervous. Of course, I was in the dark about interviews. I had no clue how to dress, and certainly didn't know what questions they were going to ask me. On the way to the interview, Grandpa role-played with me. He would ask me interview questions and I'd respond. If I needed it, which I did, he'd coach me with a better answer.

Grandpa had a great sense of humor. He was always joking around. On the day of my interview, his lightheartedness made me feel confident about the interview. He told me, "Be yourself, Shorty. Don't worry about what others think. Just answer the questions the best you can."

When we arrived, he parked in front of the building. As I walked to the restaurant's front door, the manager, a man named Edwin Gonzales, waited for me. He escorted me to a table where customers eat. After breaking the ice, he began his interrogation.

"Why should I hire you?" he asked.

That was a stumper. I did my best to sell myself.

I was so nervous, though. I was afraid he'd ask me personal questions and didn't know that he wouldn't. You know, questions like, "Where are your parents?" "Where is your Mom right now?" Because she wasn't the one who drove me to the interview. I answered the questions he did ask the best I could, and tried to be brief about it. It went something like this.

"Well," I said, "I'm not your average fifteen-year-old girl. I'm a high achiever and know what I want. I'll give this job everything I got." In other words, I let him know he wouldn't be disappointed if he hired me. It was as if The Man Upstairs had given me all the right words to say.

Next, he asked me, "Why do you want a job at such a young age?"

I said, "Because I want nice things. I want to be able to buy things I want."

Then he asked, "Where do you see yourself in five years?"

"I'm planning to get a degree and work myself through school."

"Are you planning to work after school?" And on it went. It lasted maybe a half hour, and I kept the answers basic and vague while attempting to answer honestly.

As the store manager came to the end of his questioning, he thanked me for coming in and said he would call me if I was hired. I walked out of the interview feeling like a millions bucks. I might have even been a little too confident.

Back in the car, Grandpa asked how it went. I told him it was easy. I felt like I was going to get the job.

Grandpa downplayed it. It felt like he was being a Debby Downer. I didn't expect that. He wasn't normally that way.

"Well, Shorty," he said, "Don't be disappointed if you don't get the job. It's only your first interview."

I knew he was right. I said, "You're right, Grandpa. If it's meant to be, he'll call me. If it's not, that's fine too."

My first interview and I felt I nailed it. I was going to get this job and prove Grandpa wrong. Little did I know, he was prepping me in case I didn't get the job. The next day, I waited patiently by the phone for a call from that store manager. I just knew he was going to hire me. We had a rotary phone on the wall, and I sat underneath that phone on the floor for hours waiting for it to ring.

It didn't ring.

If you haven't figured it out by now, I'm as determined as they come. I could not wait patiently. I called Taco Bell and asked to speak to the manager. He was not in. I called about five more times that day. Each time, the assistant manager informed me the manager was not in. She told me to stop calling. "If we hire you, we'll call you."

What did she mean, "We'll call you?" I mean, come on, *I cant wait forever.*

I got the sense she was trying to get rid of me. The manager was probably there but busy doing something and the assistant manager thought she could just brush me off. That's what I thought.

I asked Grandpa what he thought I should do.

"Shorty, you need to be patient," he said. "It's only been a day." The next day, he'd say, "It's only been two days." Each day, he encouraged me to be patient. But I was thinking I was likely not to get hired, or he'd have called me already. I started to wonder if I should keep looking for a job.

57

If I didn't get the job at Taco Bell, I knew I'd have to keep looking until someone took a chance and hired me. That would have been torture. I waited impatiently another day and called again. Surprisingly, I got the manager on the phone. Our conversation went something like this:

"I like the way you interviewed," he said, "but you are young and seem too good to be true. And a little too desperate."

Desperate?

"I'm not desperate," I reacted. "I'm eager to work. Is that something you don't find very often?"

It's funny to me now, but he said, "Well, to be honest, it's a little weird that you want a job so badly at fifteen. You should be out playing hopscotch with your friends."

I was in shock. There I was, right in his face, eager to work, and he was questioning my motivation. I immediately went into sales mode again.

"If you don't hire me, you're going to regret it. I will be the hardest worker you've ever had." On that note, I hung up the phone.

After cooling off, I thought to myself, *What got into me? Really? "I'll be the hardest worker you've ever had*!?"

I sure as heck believed it. I told Grandpa he was right. I should have listened to him.

"The only reason I was so negative," he said, "is because I didn't want to see you get rejected and be upset."

A few days passed and I was over it. I started looking elsewhere. Then, the Taco Bell manager called. He said he'd thought about it and wanted to give me a chance. He told me to report to work the next morning at nine a.m. I paused, taken aback. "Joni? Are you there?" I could hear the concern in his voice. He wanted to know if I was ready to accept the position.

"Yes! Yes!" I blurted it out. "I will be there bright and early."

I hung up and told Grandpa, "We did it! Taco Bell hired me." It was the best day ever.

Mom worked constantly and didn't have a lot of time to talk about things. That night, I was worried. I was going to have to explain to her how I got my worker's permit and have to be at work the next morning. How was I going to do that?

Grandpa took me home early and I made hamburgers for Mom and me. When she got home, she was surprised. I think she was relieved. She didn't have to cook.

"I have some good news for you," I said as we sat down to eat.

She was curious. She probably thought I was going to tell her I got a good grade on a school paper, or something like that. Instead, I told her Grandpa helped me get my worker's permit.

"Okay, but make sure you understand where your priorities are," she said.. "School comes first. And you know I'm not going to be able to take you back and forth to work."

"I know," I said. "Grandpa said he'd do it." Then I told her I got a job.

She was shocked at first. I got a worker's permit and a job? Then she said, "I'm happy for you, Joni, but if it interferes with school, you'll have to quit the job."

The support wasn't overwhelming, but she wasn't dead set against me having the job. I was somewhat frustrated at the less than one hundred percent support and enthusiasm. But I also understood that she wanted me to focus on the most important things first. She was being a mom. I couldn't blame her for that, but I wished she was as supportive of my passion as she was of Joey's.

Still, I was on cloud nine. It was like I had won the lottery.

Choice Points:

- Put your best foot forward - Life is all about putting your best foot forward. It's something we all have to do. No matter the situation in life, whatever you are facing, give it your best.

- Have follow-through - Trusting the process for results doesn't mean you do nothing. I got the job at Taco Bell because I had the initiative to follow through. If I hadn't been persistent in calling the manager to speak to him directly, I'd have never been able to talk myself into getting the job. A lot of people would have given up. Don't ever give up. If you want it, persistently go after it until you get it.

- Persistence pays off - Many companies fail because decision makers give up easily and are not willing to go the extra mile in achieving success. Business leaders who face their fears and obstacles head on are people who establish and grow the most profitable, effective businesses.

- Create your own opportunities- If you give up as soon as you face a hurdle, you could miss out on a wide range of opportunities. Many of your best opportunities will come after minor victories. Some of the biggest discoveries, inventions, and breakthroughs take place after a difficult situation was resolved. Be aware that your next big opportunity may be closer than you think. You could be creating it yourself.

THE CHOICE IS YOURS: TEACH YOUR CHILDREN

"Children must be taught how to think, not what to think." — Margaret Mead

I got up real early the next day. Grandma liked to make Malt-o-Meal for breakfast. She always stressed the importance of eating a healthy meal in the morning before work or school. After breakfast, Grandpa drove me to work. I was nervous and wondered what I would be asked to do. *Will the other employees like me?*

The manager greeted me with a smile. He gave me a tour of the restaurant and a uniform to wear. I was a little intimidated.

My coworkers were mostly men. An older lady and I were the only female employees. And Spanish was the dominant language amongst the staff. I thought, *How am I going to understand what they want?*

My grandparents' primary language was Spanish. That's what they spoke at home, so I was able to pick up some familiar words from the Taco Bell employees. I wasn't fluent in Spanish, even though I had taken classes at school, but I could understand some of it. Nevertheless, I was nervous about working in an environment where virtually no one else spoke English. I asked the manager what I'd be doing.

Essentially, my job was to make sure the front of the store was clean all the time, make sure the bathrooms were clean, restock the food items in the kitchen, and to ensure napkins, plates, plastic eating utensils, and paper cups were fully stocked. It didn't matter to me what the job was as long as I got paid.

I focused on my list of desires. First on the list was school clothes. Clothes I could choose for myself.

Taco Bell wasn't the most appealing place to work. At times, some of my classmates came in and ate with their parents. Then they made fun of me at school.

I made a whopping $5.00 an hour, but it felt good to have my own money. It was worth it to endure the ribbing. By the end of the summer, I had saved almost six hundred dollars.

I'd love to say working at Taco Bell was a great experience. It was male dominant, and the men were not very friendly. They often talked about me in Spanish. They didn't know I understood just enough Spanish to understand what they were saying. Things like, "Why's this girl working here? She's too young. She should be at home."

I found it intimidating.

At times, they would order me around, telling me I didn't do something right. Other times, they'd condesendingly demonstrate how to perform the simplest task, like sprinkling cheese on a taco. They were very direct in the way they spoke to me. I think they wanted me to quit.

Driving home after work, I vented to Grandpa about how horrible those men were. He would, in his typical fashion, give me advice on how to handle it.

He'd tell me to ignore them. Not to lash out. One of my favorite pieces of advice was, "One word brings another." That meant if I said something, they'd say something back. A situation can escalate.

Summer finally came to an end and it was time to go back to school. Working a real job and earning my own income gave me a new perspective on life. I appreciated everything Mom had done for Joey and me. I could not imagine what she went through working two jobs to support us. I respected her a lot more for that.

Though I was belittled for working at Taco Bell by fellow students at school—they called me "Burrito Queen,"—I wanted to continue working throughout the school year. I asked the manager if it would be okay to work some days after school and on weekends. He agreed to keep me on the schedule.

I soon graduated from cleaning tables and taking out the trash to working the drive-through.

Taco Bell was my starting point. Once I knew I could earn my own money, I wanted more. Two or three months into it, I was ready for a new challenge. The next summer, I applied for a job at Parks and Recreation.

They were hiring for a kids summer camp. How great would it be to get paid to play? The thought of it excited me.

When I was hired on, I worked with children from kindergarten through sixth grade, coordinating sporting events and games. They put me in charge of the softball games. I loved it.

I have to say, that was one of my best first jobs ever. Making my own money and not having to rely on my mother to buy me things she couldn't afford felt really good. It taught me some responsibility and, to some extent, independence. Joey would often ask to borrow money from me to buy video games or something else he thought was cool, but I was stingy with my money. It took a lot to make five hundred dollars at age fifteen. I was not about to spend it on foolish things.

I wasn't proud. I mean, Taco Bell? There's nothing sexy about that. When I tell people today that I worked at Taco Bell at fifteen, they smirk and giggle. But you know what? A job is a job. You have put your ego aside and do what is best for your family. It gave me a thick skin. I had to deal with people who were rude to me. I wanted to be somewhere else, but I learned how to deal with difficult people.

When I got my driver's permit at sixteen, I wanted a car. Mom told me she didn't have the money to buy me a car so I was going to have to do it on my own. I started saving money right away. I bought some things, but I saved a lot because I really wanted a car.

There was an auction in Santa Fe, and Grandpa said, "*Mija*, let's go look at cars." So he took me to the auction. I hadn't saved enough money to buy a vehicle yet, but I thought we were just looking. In fact, he told me, "We're just looking. We're not going to buy anything."

We went to the auction and I saw a red Honda Civic. I fell in love with it. "Grandpa, I want that car!"

"I don't think we have enough money for that," he said, "but at least I know what you like."

I begged him. "Grandpa, I'll pay you back. Will you get it for me?"

He bid on the car. But someone else outbid us. That disappointed me, but Grandpa remained positive. "We're just here to look, *Mija*. Remember, we didn't come to buy." Then, a little bit later we saw a beautiful turquoise Mercury Tracer. It had a black bra on the front, and Grandpa said, "*Mija*, this is a really nice car." They wanted fifty-five hundred dollars for it. "This one will be good for you," he said, and he bought that car. "I will front you the money and you can pay me back over time."

I did pay Grandpa back, every penny, and it taught me something about responsibility. I want to pass that on to my children.

Choice Points:

- Teach your children about responsibility from an early age - I talk to Lucas and Mila about responsibility often. I also talk to them about character. I assign them chores and pay them $1.00 per year they've been born every two weeks. They also have bank accounts, and when they want something— like toys and games—we go to the bank, they withdraw their money, and they buy what they want. Both my mom and Shawn's mom have criticized me for this, but I am adamant about teaching my children to care for themselves. Perhaps if Mom had done this when Joey and I were children, Joey might have taken a different path. Mom did, at least, teach me the value of hard work. For that, I am eternally grateful. And Grandpa taught me how to be responsible with money, how to value good things in life, and how to buy a car. Those are all things I want to pass on to Lucas and Mila.

- Model success before your children - Whatever you want your children to learn, you should model it. So many parents preach to their children then fail to practice what they preach. My children see a successful woman. They see me working hard. They see me model the behavior that I teach them, and I believe they'll be more responsible and successful adults because of it.

- Allow your children to make mistakes - Children, like adults, learn through failure. It's hard to refrain from stepping in and fixing things so that they avoid the consequences of poor choices, but poor choices are tremendous teaching tools.

- Give your children options - Even if a choice is of little consequence, kids will feel empowered if they get to make decisions for themselves. Letting go can feel uncomfortable. However, watching your children make brilliant choices later in life is worth all the uncomfortable moments along the way.

THE CHOICE IS YOURS: TOUGH LOVE

"Tough love is real love. Why? Because it's never easy. It hurts the giver far more than the receiver." — Bobby Miller

Demons. Once they get into you, it's hard to shake them loose. You're constantly fighting them off.

As a teenager, I had doubts that I could be anything other than what my father and brother were. That thought plagued my mind constantly. I felt that I wasn't worthy to be anything else. The dysfunction had taken over. When addiction is core to your family identity, it's easy to fall into its trap.

As I grew older, the family dysfunction worsened. For the most part, my father was out of the picture. He couldn't function if he wasn't on heroin. He had lost everything, including his children. And he didn't care.

He moved in with his mother and father in Roswell, effectively making himself their problem. My grandparents simply accepted that they would share the addicted life with him. They spent their retirement taking care of him. They made excuses for him, bailed him out of situations he had gotten himself into, and generally catered to his every need. It looked to me as if they were vicariously living his life for him.

Other family members, seeing the pattern in Joseph's and Joey's lives, must have thought that I would follow in those footsteps. It was natural to think that way, and I'd hear them say things like, "Joni's going to be just like them."

I'd deny it. But it was a struggle.

I didn't understand. I wanted so badly to shake Joseph of his addiction. Heroin had taken over, and I knew it. There wasn't going to be a way out unless he decided to overcome it himself. It was a sad thing to see.

We all make choices. Joseph chose to destroy himself. His parents chose to enable him. I chose to fight the battle of the demons and pave my own path.

Not only did my father throw away his own life, but he also ruined the lives of his parents. They were afraid of losing him and dedicated themselves to caring for him. They shot their retirement dreams away babysitting their dysfunctional adult son.

Even sadder, Joey repeated the cycle.

My parents' divorce affected him emotionally. I'm not sure he ever got over it. For starters, there was a gaping hole where a father figure had once been. He was five years old when they divorced, a year older than me, so his recollection of Joseph's presence in our lives would be a bigger memory for him than for me. Plus, as a boy, the lack of a father figure had a deeper impact on him than on me. I can't imagine what it did to him to have his father uprooted at an early age. It must have been devastating.

Meanwhile, Mom enabled Joey, bailing him out of trouble, and making excuses for him. One of her favorites was, "He doesn't have a father figure." As if that automatically led to bad choices.

The truth is, we had Pops. He adopted us, but by then, Joey was in high school. He'd already established the trajectory of his life. Even though our stepfather was a great man who stuck by Mom and her children through thick and thin, Joey couldn't see it. He didn't want to.

Pops was big on rules. He was not a strict disciplinarian, but he believed in rules, and if you lived in his house, you were going to follow the rules.

One time, when Pops tried to discipline Joey for breaking the rules, Pops wanted to hold him accountable, Mom played her trump card. She begged Pops to leave Joey alone, claiming he didn't have a father figure.

Pops lost it. "Well, I *am* his father figure!" He reiterated the need for discipline, but added that he and Mom should be on the same page. Undivided.

They argued. It was a big fight too. Yelling, screaming, cursing. They didn't get physical, but their passions rose to a pitch. Pops, frustrated and angry, stormed out of the house, yelling something like, "If you're not going to let me discipline my son the way I want to discipline him, then I'm not sticking around!" And he was gone.

I thought it was permanent. I thought for sure he was out of our lives and not coming back. I had already lost one father and I thought I was losing another one. I was in the eighth grade at the time.

Pops and I had grown close. I mean, he was my stepfather, and the only real father I ever knew. When he walked out, I got mad at Mom.

"Look at what you've done, Mom," I said, stifling the tears. "Because you baby Joey, you're going to lose your husband. And I'm not going to have a father." I ran to my room and locked the door.

We all had been telling her she was enabling Joey—Grandpa, Pops, and me. Eventually, it would sink in, but not on that day.

Pops loved us and wanted to do right for the whole family. I got into trouble in high school once and he got onto me. I deserved it.

By that time, Shawn and I were dating. I was invited to a party with some friends and Shawn was out of town. My girlfriends were drinking and I wanted to have fun, so I joined them. We were drinking Peach Schnapps and I had too much. Shawn had some friends at the party who noticed and drove me back to my grandparents' house. They walked me up to the door and rang the doorbell, then left me there so they didn't have to get into it with Joey. Then Joey took care of me all night.

He said I'd feel better if I drank some milk. I didn't feel better. I threw up. All night long, I was spewing Peach Schnapps and milk. It upset my grandparents.

"Joni, I can't believe you did this," Grandma said.

Grandpa agreed. The next morning, they asked me to leave. Grandpa delivered the message. "You're not allowed to stay here anymore," he said. So Joey drove me to Mom's house.

Mom was livid. She couldn't even look at me. But Pops kept his cool and talked to me about it.

"Actions have consequences," he said. And because Mom couldn't deal with it, he was the one who showed me some tough love. He grounded me. It was one of the few times I've ever been grounded for anything. I respected Pops for that.

Choice Points:

- Everything you do has consequences - Pops taught me that everything has consequences. Some are good and some are bad. Whatever you do in life, be prepared to pay the consequences.

- If you do it, own it - Being responsible means owning your decisions. Good ones and bad ones.

- Show some tough love - Loving someone doesn't mean excusing their behavior. Sometimes, you have to show some tough love. That could mean punishing bad behavior. It could mean a harsh word or two. If it strengthens the person who needs it, that's what matters. Don't be afraid to show tough love, but understand that it's not something you'll have to do all the time. It will be more effective if you use it sparingly. Pops understood that.

THE CHOICE IS YOURS: GUARD YOUR DREAMS

"You either face the fear and conquer it or face the fact that you'll always be where you are now. You can't expect to get somewhere different if you keep driving down the same road—You have TO CHANGE YOUR PATH!" – Stacy Estolas

Joey was searching for something he couldn't find. When he turned twenty-two, he met a girl named Shelly. A few months later, they were married. But they weren't the most ideal couple. They were both feisty. Together, they were like a hurricane. They fought most of the time, and their fights usually ended in jabs. It wasn't Joey doing the punching.

One evening, Joey showed up at my parents' house. He and his new wife had had a huge fight. She had busted several beer bottles over his head. He was bleeding profusely. I thought he was going to need serious medical attention.

A year went by and they were still together. The fighting was constant. It seemed like they had a huge fight that got physical about once a month. I was in college by then, living life on my own terms, carrying around my own baggage. Joey's drama took center stage in the family, keeping everyone busy.

It was during this time that Joey started using drugs heavily. He was dealing and using, a habit which added fuel to the fire. Their fights grew more intense. Their mutual abuse led to domestic violence disputes. Both landed in jail multiple times. As she had many other times before, Mom was there to bail Joey out of jail.

Every. Single. Time.

What's more, Shelly's father was the male version of Mom. He'd bail Shelly out.

Joey and Shelly eventually parted ways. Shelly took the house, which left Joey homeless. Mom bailed him out again. She gave him a place to stay. I knew it was a bad idea.

I had seen what happened with my father and his parents. It could have ended up the same way, with Mom pissing away her retirement to babysit her dysfunctional adult son. Shawn and I had our own idea.

My first year of college was a difficult year. I had moved in with Shawn, now my husband. We discussed Joey moving in with us. Shawn thought Joey might see how awesome our life was together and hoped it might rub off.

It didn't work out that way. Joey was a difficult housemate.

I was resistant from the start. Shawn grew up in a close family, so he was much more amenable to the idea of family helping family. But he didn't know what he was asking for. I told Shawn I didn't think we should take him in. "Let him suffer the consequences of his own decisions."

"But he's your brother," Shawn said. "He asked *me* for help."

"That's not going to be a good thing for our relationship," I said. "I know Joey, and it's just going to last a short time before he loses his grip."

"If we don't do it, will you regret it?" Shawn asked.

I thought about it and decided, yeah, I would. I'd probably feel guilty for the rest of my life if I didn't at least try to help Joey.

Shawn suggested we let him move in with us. "If he's around us more, that will help him overcome his bad habits."

"Well, you do what you want," I said, not fully convinced, "but I'm telling you that you should let him do his own thing."

I finally halfheartedly agreed. But deep down, I knew it wasn't going to work. I felt like Joey needed to turn himself into the police if he had got himself in trouble with the law. And I wasn't sure that he hadn't.

Still, Shawn was adamant. I think he felt guilty even considering not helping, because Joey was family. He told me later that we were helping Joey because Joey had asked him for our help and Shawn agreed.

There was an internal battle going on inside of me. On the one hand, I didn't want to say "no" to my brother. I wanted to see him happy, and I wanted good things for him, so I wanted to help him. On the other hand, I was afraid to let him into my house because I knew he hadn't changed and it was going to affect my relationship with Shawn. We had worked so hard to have a healthy relationship, but I thought if Shawn saw the real Joey, then the real me, and what our family was, he would run from it. It was an unfounded fear.

So, the demons came out in full force. They had me fearful of helping Joey when he needed it most, but the other side of me was regretting the fact that I was reluctant to help.

Joey lived like a slob. He came in all hours of the night, dragging girl after girl in and having loud sex with them in his bedroom. Shawn and I could hear it from our bedroom. And he continued to experiment with drugs. It frustrated me. All I could think about was Joey bringing one of his drug deals home, or using drugs at my house, and I had no way to control his behavior short of kicking him out.

Then it got worse. He not only walked in the door at all hours of the night, but he would sometimes call at two or three in the morning, stranded and out of gas. Shawn and I would have to go and pick him up. We felt like we were bailing him out—just like Mom had done. I finally had to draw the line. He became so comfortable living with us that he would bring random girls in and sleep with them, even if he'd just met them that night. He would arise at 2 p.m. the next day, exhausted from all-night partying and drug usage.

One early afternoon, while he was taking a shower, I went into his room and found used condoms under his bed and drugs in his pockets. I lost it.

I asked him to move out. It was, in fact, beginning to affect my relationship with Shawn, and we argued over it.

Shawn's patience was strong, but eventually he became annoyed with Joey's bad habits. Working three jobs, going to school full time, trying to pay off a mortgage and two cars, and putting food on the table was wearing me down. Shawn and I worked our butts off only to have Joey sit around all day, mooching. I finally had enough and told Joey to move out.

I felt like the worst sister in the world. How could I throw my own brother out into the streets, with nothing? It wasn't easy. But at the end of the day, I believe it was the best choice, the one I had to make.

Tough love. That was something Mom could never give to Joey. She bailed him out constantly. Whatever he got himself into, she was his plan out, and she gladly played the role. I did not want to repeat her mistakes.

It hurt to see Joey on the street, but I believed he had to hit rock bottom before bouncing back up.

And Joey didn't make it easy. He'd make me feel like crap. He'd call me and curse me up and down the wall, tell me he couldn't believe his own kin would throw him out on the street. One day, it was raining buckets, he called to say he was stranded and needed someone to pick him up. I felt guilty and gave in. I found him on the seedy side of Albuquerque, right where he said he would be.

Another time, after hours of driving street after street, up and down lanes and avenues, I couldn't find him. I went back home. He really didn't want me to find him, I realized later.

This went on for a month. Then, one day he called and said, "Joni, I'm sorry I treated you the way I did. Can I please come back and live with you?"

"Not until you seek help, Joey." I choked on the tears. "You can't come back into my home until you get help."

I hated doing it, but that was the best choice for both of us. I believe it was the only way I could help him. I had to stay firm, and it's one of the best decisions I've ever made.

At that time, Joey had several warrants for his arrest. Most were unpaid speeding tickets.

He confided to Shawn that he wanted to turn himself in.

He asked if Shawn could drive him to the police station. I said that would be okay, and we executed the plan. While Shawn drove, he and Joey had a long talk. Shawn told him that I was trying to do what was best to get him better. As they pulled into the police station, Joey reached into his pocket, pulled out some drugs, and pushed them into his mouth. Shawn, flabbergasted, asked why he was doing that to himself.

Joey told him he may as well take another hit, since he might be in the slammer a while.

It was clear that Joey wasn't ready to change. Something inside him kept him from wanting to change. Shawn and I both realized we couldn't help Joey unless he was ready to be helped. That was a choice we had to make. Unfortunately, Joey wasn't ready. He had his own demons to fight.

After that, Joey and I drifted apart. When he got out of jail three months later, I didn't try to help as much as before. If he wasn't going to help himself, I reasoned, I wasn't going to help him either.

Was I wrong? Was I selfish? At times, I felt so.

Still, kicking Joey out was one of the hardest things I've ever had to do. I love Joey unconditionally. Deep inside, I wanted to help him figure out his life. But he had to want that for himself.

"You don't want me here. Fine." Joey laid the guilt trip on me hard. "I'll just take my trash bag and put all my clothes in it and walk the streets." And he did. Before he left, he said, "If you want to come and find me, you're more than welcome to, but I hope I don't die tonight."

Later, he called me. It was two o'clock in the morning. I was trying to sleep.

"Joni, I'm at Central. I'm freezing. Can you come and pick me up?"

I went down in my car to look for him, guilty that I was thinking about bailing him out. But I didn't want him on the streets, freezing. I knew he was playing a game and wanted me to feel sorry for him. Unfortunately, it worked.

It wasn't long before Shawn got to know Joey the way I knew him. It got to the point where we were both afraid of leaving Joey alone in the house while we were at school. What if he stole our stuff and sold it for drugs? What if he blew up the house, or something awful?

We were really stressing over it, and we'd bicker over little things. When we went to visit family, they knew something was wrong. It showed all over our faces, our body language. They noticed it. Someone would ask what's going on with us, or say something like, You two aren't acting like yourselves.

Truth is, we were trying to hide the fact that we were arguing. But we didn't hide it so well.

In those situations where Joey would leave the house and call either Shawn or me to pick him up somewhere, we felt like it was our responsibility. He was staying in our house, after all. At the same time, we felt guilty for enabling him. We wanted to make sure he got home safely. It was a battle.

Of course, he made me feel bad because he had nowhere else to go. I knew he had to find his own way, but he wanted me to bail him out like Mom would do. Eventually, I held firm. If I didn't help him, he'd call Mom and she'd come running. At the end of the day, he ended up back at Mom's house. I told her she needed to put some restrictions on him, show him some tough love. But she couldn't do it.

Choice Points:

- Don't let fear steal your dreams - What are you afraid of? Whatever it is, don't let it steal your dreams. To succeed at that, you've got to make your dreams bigger than your fears. Feed the dreams. Focus on them. Write them down. Pursue them with everything you've got.

- Don't let others dictate your future - Both enablers and the enabled often want to pull you into their nightmare. Guard your dreams from the tendency to feed on the drama.

- Don't be an enabler - Being an enabler will steal your dreams, your ambition, and your drive. It will suck life right out of you, and it doesn't help the person you're enabling. Learning not to be an enabler is not a one-time event; it's a process. Be vigilant in fighting the temptation to be an enabler.

THE CHOICE IS YOURS: HAVE FUN AND FALL IN LOVE

"To the world you may be one person, but to one person you may be the world." — Bill Wilson

Shawn and I had an instant connection. He made me believe in love at first sight. I was fifteen when we met. Twenty-three years later, we still give each other butterflies. Every day, we tell each other how grateful we are that we found each other. It's amazing to know your spouse thinks the world of you.

We met in typing class. Shawn sat in the front row. I sat in the back, on the opposite side of the room so I could get a clear view of him. I watched him like a hawk. I only knew him by association through a friend of mine at the time. But we had never talked.

One day, while Shawn was typing, I seized the opportunity to break the ice. Lucky for us, I had a bad habit of showing up to class unprepared. After the teacher assigned our work for the day, I discovered I hadn't taken any typing paper to class. So, I strolled to the front of the classroom in my blue polo shirt and Catholic schoolgirl skirt and asked Shawn if I could borrow some typing paper.

I could tell he was nervous as he reached into his book bag and pulled out a ream of typing paper. He sifted through the paper to separate a single sheet from the rest. He was so cute fumbling with the paper, his coke bottle glasses hanging gingerly on the tip of nose. Finally, he gasped and shoved the entire ream of paper into my hands.

"Here," he said sheepishly, "just take it all."

"Thanks," I said, a bit flirtatious, and bounced back to my desk at the back of the room.

A few minutes later, Shawn walked to the back of the room and asked me, "I gave you all my paper. Mind if I borrow some of it back?"

I laughed, handed him some paper, and returned to my assignment.

That's how we finally met. It was apparent to me that if I didn't make the first move, it was never going to happen.

Shawn was a member of the soccer team, and I was a cheerleader. A few days later, after one of his games, someone on the team hosted a party. Shawn and I were both there, hanging out at the bonfire. Shawn tried to hide under his hat, but I wouldn't let him. We talked a little bit, but it was a couple of days later when I asked him out. "Hey," I said, "what do you think about going to a movie?"

He couldn't resist the offer. After that, we were a permanent fixture. We'd meet at his locker between classes and pass notes back and forth to each other in class.

When St. Michael's had its homecoming, he asked me to go. I eagerly accepted. I was new to high school, new to the Catholic school, and had my first private school boyfriend. Homecoming was a natural next step. We had a great time together, and, after homecoming, we drew closer. We hung out together every day.

One of our favorite activities was family dinner. Shawn's mom was a busy OB-GYN, busy enough to not have time for cooking. They ate out a lot and Shawn would invite me to go out to dinner with them.

Within a few weeks, Shawn and I had grown so close he wanted to spend more time with me than with his family. We started skipping family dinners. His mom didn't take that well and asked him why he was spending so much time with me.

Of course, Shawn was her first son. And he had never spent much time with others outside of the family, being so shy. He certainly hadn't had a lot of girlfriends. That took some getting used to for his mom.

We watched a lot of movies together. But there was one event in Albuquerque that caught my eye. I asked Shawn if he'd be interested. He was shocked. After all, what kind of a girl likes monster trucks?

I did. Watching monster trucks was something Joey and I got into together. Because I was always trying to be like my bigger brother, I got into them too. I turned Shawn onto monster trucks.

He, in turn, got me interested in Whirlwind Weekend. His family would go to Albuquerque for a weekend. They'd go to water parks, amusement parks, and do other fun stuff together.

One weekend, there was a monster truck rally on the same weekend as Whirlwind Weekend. Shawn wanted to go to the monster truck event with me. His mom got livid over it, asking if he was going to miss Whirlwind Weekend for a girl.

Shawn defended himself valiantly. Yes, he was going to miss the family weekend for a girl. But not just any girl. We were getting to be very good friends by that point. He'd take me to music concerts, movies, and monster truck rallies. We'd hang out at the park and talk. We were a couple. Once it happened, there was no splitting us up.

Before I knew it, Shawn had become my best friend. We could talk about anything. Because I had trust issues, I was selective about who my friends were, and Shawn had won my heart.

I wasn't easy to get to know. I'd built such a thick wall that even my closest friends didn't know my most intimate secrets.

To this day, my best high school girl friend doesn't know about my family's history with drug addiction and how that led to fear and insecurity. But Shawn knew. He was the only one I could ever open up with. There was just something about him that made me feel comfortable sharing things I couldn't share with anyone else—even my mom.

I believe everything happens for a reason. Shawn and I were meant to be together. Our relationship wasmutually beneficial from the start. We didn't realize how much we were helping each other grow until it happened. And if we hadn't found each other, it's possible one or both of us would have walked a different path. I'd probably be wearing scrubs and sticking thermometers in little kids' mouths. Or working as an emergency room nurse.

Shawn helped me in so many ways. For starters, he helped me overcome my fears. He was always encouraging and supportive.

Never judgmental. Fear of being judged kept me from sharing my story with anyone other than Shawn. Some people might say I was fake, or not true to myself, but I had issues to face. Shawn helped me face them.

Fear of rejection is another thing Shawn helped me overcome. I've always known I was going to be somebody. But I was still afraid I'd follow the path of Joey or my father. I feared others rejecting me on account of my family's dysfunction.

Oh, my gosh, can this be genetic? I often thought to myself. *Is it in my DNA? Am I going to end up like them?* The demons can really play with your mind.

Shawn pushed me past my comfort zone. No matter what I faced, he would challenge me to face it head on. When I was picked on by the girls on the softball team, I wanted to quit. Shawn talked me through it, encouraging me to persevere. Not to let them win. Because of him, I did, and I made the varsity team every year of high school.

There were times when I'd open up and talk about Joey, my father, the family dysfunction. Just talking about it made me upset. When I'd break down and cry, Shawn would console me. That allowed me to open up more. Slowly, the wall was breaking down.

If you asked Shawn, he would say I helped him. I helped him come out from under his hat.

As a child, he was the poster child of low self-esteem. His coke bottle glasses made him a target for bullies. Sports became his medicine. They developed in him the value of hard work and persistence. They also gave him the early impetus for overcoming his confidence issues. There were times, he confided in me, when his coaches were mean, even disrespectful, to him. But he pressed on, determined to never give up. When other boys quit, Shawn persisted. It gained my admiration. I didn't know anyone in my family with those qualities. It made Shawn even more attractive to me.

While growing up, a good day for Shawn was going unnoticed. He would hide his face under a hat and make himself a shadow. Like an Untouchable. He couldn't make eye contact with anybody, fearing what they might think of him. Being around me helped him overcome his social anxiety. He would eventually feel more comfortable in social situations.

Bottom line, Shawn helped me get over my fears and I helped him get over his. It was a win-win. We had each other's backs all the way through high school.

Shawn was ahead by one year. He graduated in 1999 and was quickly accepted to a few colleges. He wanted to be a mechanical engineer, so his top picks were the University of Colorado and the University of Michigan where they had strong engineering programs. I encouraged him to choose the college that would help him reach his goals. He wanted to be close to me.

I told not to stick around just for me. If our relationship was to be, our paths would reconnect at some point in the future. I sincerely believed that.

We had been dating for three years, so we were really close. It would have been hard doing my last year of school with Shawn at a distance, but I wanted him to follow his dreams. I didn't want him to have regrets later if he made the wrong choice, so I tried to be supportive and encouraging. I wanted him to do what was best for his career. I began to prepare myself for the eventuality that he would attend an out-of-state college.

"Why don't you come with me?" He asked one day. We had been talking about it for a while, so he just spit it out. "Whatever college I choose, come with me."

"I'm not sure," I said. I was in my last year of high school, after all. And I still had to choose a college for myself, because I was planning to go into nursing. "I'm not just going to follow you. I have to see where my path leads."

I knew I was likely to attend a university in New Mexico. The state had a program that gave students with a 2.5 high school grade point average a full scholarship if they went to a New Mexico university. I knew I wouldn't get a scholarship for an out-of-state university.

Shawn considered with whether to pursue his education out of state or beat me to an in-state university. He ultimately chose the

University of New Mexico (UNM) and took advantage of the lottery scholarship. He loathed having to tell his mom.

Education was very important to his family, especially his mom. They had a big fight about his decision. His parents had saved $60,000 toward Shawn's college education. He could have gone anywhere he wanted.

Deep down, I was glad Shawn made the choice he had. It meant he'd be near me. After all, he was my best friend.

One year later, I entered UNM. Shawn and I were in school together again.

Choice Points:

- Don't be selfish - Loving someone doesn't mean being selfish. It means wishing the best for them. Shawn and I look out for each other by wanting the best for the other. By focusing on what is best for each other, our relationship is stronger. We both get what we want and need, and each of us are stronger individually as a result.

- Do what's right for your relationship – and have fun doing it! - Relationships are forged in the everyday events of your lives. Where they intersect. Just as you don't live your individual life for everyone else, you don't manage your relationships for everyone else. Shawn and I did what was best for us, even in the early stages of our relationship. It didn't always make our parents happy, but Shawn and I were building our future together. We had to do what was right for us. And we made sure we had fun doing it.

- Have a direction - Shawn and I have always been honest with each other. We had separate goals and dreams, but God put us together then forged a single path for us. As John Lennon once said, "Life is what happens while you are busy making other plans." So have a plan, set some goals, and see where that takes you. You'll likely end up some place else, and that's okay.

THE CHOICE IS YOURS: START EARLY AND FINISH STRONG

"There are two mistakes one can make along the road to truth. ..
Not going all the way and not starting." — Buddha

Shawn was frugal. He was so frugal that he rented an apartment on Albuquerque's Central Avenue, well known for being a war zone. There were drug deals everywhere, and gangs. Several times, we witnessed Shawn's bus driver get into it with homeless people. Shawn's parents tried to steer him in another direction, but he was adamant he wanted to live in the cheap part of town.

All he wanted was a bedroom. He'd walk down the street to catch a bus rather than drive because he didn't want to buy a parking permit from the college. That's how frugal he was.

Shawn's next door neighbor was a drug dealer whose girlfriend had just got out of prison. One day, they asked Shawn if he would drive them to a friend's house. Shawn obliged. It was a weekend and I happened to be visiting. When we arrived, Shawn and I sat in the car while Shawn's neighbor worked a drug deal right before our eyes. That was unexpected.

Despite being in the seedy part of town, Cinnamon Tree was one of the nicest apartment complexes in the area. When he was in his apartment, Shawn kept the door locked because he didn't want to have to act like Bruce Willis if a neighbor wigged out. He wasn't itching to die hard.

Still, his apartment was well-decorated. His mom had some mad interior decorating skills. She hung family photos on the wall, a Georgia O'Keefe painting, added curtains and linens, and gave it a woman's touch. She made it feel homey, down to two leather couches.

Rent for Shawn's one-bedroom apartment was three hundred fifty dollars. His annual living expenses amounted to seven thousand dollars. That impressed me. To curb expenses, he ate at Taco Bell, and had dinner at my mom's house. When I graduated high school a year later, I moved in.

I knew it wouldn't go well with my family. But I was ready to be on my own. Mom was focused on Joey and I bounced back and forth from her house to Grandpa's. I felt like I was already on my own. In fact, I didn't spend a lot of time at Grandpa's that last year of school because Shawn and I were spending so much time together.

Grandma and I were really close. If I shared something with her before talking to Mom, she'd tell me what she thought about it respectfully and confidentially. So, she was the first person I told.

I expected her to be against it, being a strict conservative Catholic. But she had nothing negative to say, which shocked me.

The church's official doctrine is "marriage first." But I figured my grandparents probably knew "shacking up" was coming. Mom did it with my father, and that might have been why it was no surprise to them.

She said, Knowing my mom, she wouldn't approve. Grandma was trying to prepare me for the backlash.

"I'd like to have your support," I told her. And I really did want her as my advocate when I told mom.

Not long afterward, Shawn and I invited his parents and mine to dinner. That should have been a clue right there because that was something we didn't do. We were either with my family or his, but not both together.

We went to one of our favorite restaurants, Tomasita's. I could tell by everyone's body language that they knew something was up. We ate dinner—Shawn's parents, my parents, Grandma, and Shawn and me (Grandpa didn't want to be involved)—and afterward, Shawn and I broke the news.

My parents didn't say much. Shawn's parents were disappointed, especially his mom, who was a well-known and respected doctor in Santa Fe. His dad owned a cabinet shop. They were very clear that they were against us moving in together. They wanted him to pursue his engineering career first. Being strong Methodists, they were very traditional. Plus, Shawn's mom was overprotective and considered him too young to be playing house.

The first year was tough. Shawn wanted to include his parents in every decision about our shared living space. He really respected his parents.

You could say he was born with a silver spoon in his mouth. They would have given him anything he wanted. But to Shawn, life was more than a sweet trip to the candy shop. He wanted to earn his keep. He wanted to work his way to getting what he wanted. Even if his parents fronted the money for something, he would work hard to pay them back. That was the kind of a person he was.

I was used to doing things on my own. My parents told me if I moved out of the house, I would have to get a job. In fall of 2000, I enrolled in the University of New Mexico to study nursing.

I had always wanted to be a nurse. Grandma's brother was mentally ill and often needed assistance, so I spent a lot of time helping her while growing up. I did a lot of things he couldn't do for himself. Grandma would say to me, You care for people like you really enjoy it. And I did, really.

My first semester at college consisted of sixteen hours of coursework. I applied for a job, as promised, at the YMCA. They hired me to take care of kids, but it wasn't enough hours to support myself. I got a second job working nights at Subway.

I'd get home at 11:00 p.m. and still had homework to do. Shawn saved money provided by his parents and worked weekends at his dad's shop. Together, we managed to make ends meet.

Not your typical college kids, we didn't party like our peers. While we were raised in two different worlds, we shared the same ambitious drive. We didn't have much of a life other than school, work, and occasionally going out to eat. Our date nights were usually spent at Taco Bell, because that was what we could afford. And we loved it when Shawn's parents came to visit because they hooked us up with good food and stocked our pantry full of groceries from Sam's Club. I gained a few pounds after my first year living with Shawn.

The Mexican food I made at home didn't help. I had mastered my mother's red chile enchilada recipe and Shawn loved it. We ate that meal at least once or twice a week.

Our preferred entertainment was relaxing in front of the television. One popular show we liked watching together was MacGyver. It gave us time to decompress.

Shawn also liked going to the movies. I wasn't a huge movie person, but he loved watching action movies. The first *Fast and Furious* movie released in 2001, so guess who became its biggest fan? Shawn and I have watched every movie in the series.

Most of the time, we were perched in front of the TV. Cop shows were our favorite. If it wasn't MacGyver, it was America's Most Wanted, CSI, or Law and Order.

Shawn was also a big fan of Family Feud, which he still watches today. And if there was a talk show or reality TV show with someone from New Mexico on it, we'd watch that. TV became our way of letting the day roll off our backs.

One day, in the fall of 2001, I retired to bed, leaving Shawn to late night TV. This particular evening, he was into an infomercial on real estate. It featured the prominent real estate investor Russ Whitney. Whitney had a little comical style, which appealed to Shawn's dry sense of humor.

When we climbed out of bed the next morning, Shawn couldn't shut up about Russ Whitney. He tried explaining to me how we could make money in real estate buying property with no down payment. I was skeptical. I thought, *No way; there is something wrong here.*

An infomercial, essentially, is a commercial that masquerades as useful information. And they always include testimonials from people who supposedly benefited from the product they're selling. You never see anyone who says, Yeah, I tried it and failed miserably. It's always, I made thousands of dollars doing this.

Being a "show me first" kind of person, I wasn't buying it.

One of the objections I had was the "no down payment" strategy. I was certain there was no way we could profit from buying properties without money. I simply couldn't believe it. My father's numerous lies, his and Joey's drug addictions, and the family dysfunction all prevented me from even considering the possibility. I possessed an *unhealthy* skepticism. Shawn, on the other hand, was excited.

As it turned out, Russ Whitney was having a one-day event in Albuquerque. It cost five hundred dollars to attend. When Shawn told me about it, I damn near wet my pants. That was a lot of money on our Taco Bell budget. To recoup that would take me at least a month, even with two jobs. Nevertheless, he talked me into it, and we went to see Russ Whitney.

I can be hard-headed. Shawn did well to prepare me for the event. He said, Just listen to him. Don't go in with a negative attitude.

And that's what I did.

I surprised myself and went in with an open mind without knowing what we were getting into. That one day event changed my life.

There were hundreds of people sitting in the ballroom of a Sheraton hotel. Lines wrapped around and out the door to see what this late-night infomercial guy had to offer. And I was thinking, *Who is this guy?* He was like a celebrity that I didn't know.

He put on a pretty good show. It wasn't MacGyver, but it was informative. And his team did a heck of a job getting the crowd fired up about real estate investing with "little or no money down." He shared some of his real estate investing tips, and other topics too. For instance, he talked about keeping a positive attitude, working hard, and "establishing the life you always wanted."

Those words were music to my ears. Who doesn't want "the life you always wanted?" At nineteen, I finally had my own song to sing. I could be successful in real estate and have the life of my dreams? Sold!

I was so fired up, I was ready to start the next day.

As a child, I constantly tried to prove my worth to someone— mostly my family—just to get them to pay attention to me. Unless I did something positive, or something they deemed "good enough," they paid no attention to me. I was praise-starved. Because of this, I spent my entire life working hard, putting myself *out there* in hopes that someone might notice me. With real estate, I didn't need to do that. If I could work hard and apply what I learned, I'd be successful.

The one-day seminar was over and, of course, the next step was to get additional training. We were flat broke college students. I thought to myself, *How in the world are we going to afford these courses?* What really caught my eye was Russ Whitney's package deal: Five bootcamps in various cities throughout the year. Additionally, we'd get a mentor to come to our own city and teach us, walk us through how to close real estate deals, and answer all of our questions. The cost of that package was a whopping $20,000.

I almost threw up in my mouth. How in the world could two broke college kids afford that?

Excited to get our real estate career up and going, we could not get back home soon enough and use the techniques we learned from the Russ Whitney workshop. The first thing we did was look for a local Realtor who could show us some properties. That would allow us to get familiar with the market.

A week later, we were making offers on properties. Low and behold, we had one accepted. Now what?

We had no money to buy the property. Most people would have this part figured out before they made offers. Not me. I create problems first, then figure out how to solve them. Call me naïve or stupid, but that's how I did it. I mean, what's the point in trying to figure it out first? We didn't know a thing about real estate. It could take years to figure out. I didn't have years! I wanted the life of my dreams *right now.*

While trying to figure out how we were going to buy our first property, we applied for a credit card. After being approved, we used that credit card to pay for our first property. Shawn got a $5,000 cash advance on the credit card and we used it to make a down payment on a house.

When we told his mom, she blew up. "Why would you buy a house with a credit card?"

"Well," Shawn said, "We gotta start somewhere."

We never even took ownership of the property. We already had the buyer lined up. On closing day, we got our twelve thousand dollars, paid off the credit card, and kept the rest. As crazy as it sounds, I wouldn't recommend using a credit card to purchase real estate. But that's what we did. We haven't looked back.

I bought my first real property at nineteen. This poor girl who grew up in a trailer park in Tesuque, New Mexico, barely making it through childhood, suddenly was a real estate investor. I couldn't have been prouder. My hustle and drive got stronger.

Shawn's parents had saved up some college money that he didn't use due to receiving his scholarship. That meant he could use that money on something else. So he spent it on real estate courses. But we had to get permission from his parents and his mom flipped her lid. After some discussion, and a little arguing, we persuaded them to let us use that money for the $20,000 Russ Whitney course.

When we attended the first bootcamp, called "Driving For Dollars," we learned all about wholesaling. If you don't want to spend a lot of money on marketing, just drive neighborhoods. When you see an ugly house, research it, find out who the owner is, and, if it's vacant, make an offer. So, we did that. And once we got a house under contract, we flipped it to another investor who would make the needed repairs. We never even took possession of the property.

Eventually, we'd invest in bandit signs. Those are the little yard signs you see scattered around neighborhoods during election seasons. Real estate investors call them "bandit signs" because local municipalities often have ordinances that restrict their usage, but those are often ignored. Ours said, "Joni Buys Houses." We thought having a woman's name on the signs would make people feel more comfortable, less fearful. It worked. Our purple stop sign-looking bandit signs got us a lot of business.

I hit the second decade of my life in stride. Twenty years old, a student at the University of New Mexico, a waitress at TGI Fridays, and a real estate dabbler. Then I quit school, got my real estate license, and pursued a full-time real estate career.

I really didn't care for school to begin with. I was never good at it. It just wasn't for me. I only went to college because I knew how important it was to my family. Had I finished, I'd have been the first in my family to complete a college education.

My parents weren't happy either, and neither were Shawn's. In fact, Shawn's parents blamed him for my decision to quit school. Shawn's mom said, "You're the one who wanted the real estate career, not Joni."

Boy, were they wrong. I was totally into it.

It didn't matter what we said to them, they thought our real estate business was just a hobby. Neither of our parents praised us for my decision to quit school, or to go into real estate. Shawn's mom was dead set on him becoming an engineer. I don't think my parents cared what I did as long as I stayed out of trouble. They were so occupied with what Joey was doing they didn't have time to praise me for my accomplishments.

I believe this is one of the reasons Shawn and I are successful today. Neither of us received any praise from our parents, so we just drove ourselves to success.

I was the negotiator, Shawn the calculator. I could talk to people and liked doing it. Shawn was analytical, doing the math, making sure the deals were financially sound. If it looked good on paper, I'd wheel and deal. We made a great team.

Our first mentor was a man named Mark Wilder. He was a part of the Russ Whitney program and he taught us everything we knew about wholesaling. If it wasn't for him, we wouldn't have gone far in real estate. When the market turned in 2005, we took an interest in pre-foreclosures.

Foreclosures were peaking. It was the height of the financial crisis when a lot of people lost their homes and foreclosures were peaking. We were there to help some of those people get out of their mortgages without destroying their credit.

We started by creating our own foreclosure list. We'd go down to the courthouse, get a list of people in foreclosure, and knock on doors. But New Mexico is a judicial state, so foreclosures had to go through the court system before they could be finalized. It's a very lengthy process that can take as long as two years.

We built our business by knocking on doors and buying houses from people going through that process.

There was an internet radio show at the time called Creative Real Estate Online. Shawn listened to this program while working as a part-time bookkeeper for his dad's cabinet shop business. One of the guests on the show was a man named Charles Fuller. He and his wife worked together on pre-foreclosures and were looking for partners.

Shawn thought that was cool. So, he called the man. Charles flew from Texas to New Mexico to meet Shawn and me. He told us he could help us buy pre-foreclosures, show us the ropes, and hold our hand along the way.

Shawn and I agreed that we'd love to have another mentor.

So the Fullers helped us buy our first pre-foreclosure in Albuquerque. After that, we became regular partners. Shawn and I located the properties and made the buying and selling arrangements. The Fullers provided the money. We split the profits. Over time, Shawn and I put our money into the deals and took a bigger piece of the cut. Eventually, we were getting 80 percent and the Fullers were getting 20 percent.

Choice Points:

- Watch how you spend your money - Frugality is a virtue. So many people just throw money away. I respected Shawn, and still do, for being so frugal while in college. His frugality taught me to watch where every dollar goes. Don't spend more money than you can earn. Invest it early for the biggest returns.

- Be teachable - Shawn and I knew nothing about real estate, but we were willing to learn. When you have some knowledgeable person ready and willing to teach you the skills you need to be successful, take advantage of that opportunity.

- Learn the art of the pivot - Markets don't stay the same. Keep your eye on the direction of the market and learn to pivot when it makes sense.

THE CHOICE IS YOURS: WORK HARD AND BE WISE

"Far and away the best prize that life has to offer is the chance to work hard at work worth doing." — Theodore Roosevelt

By the time I was twenty-three, our careers had taken off. Shawn and I were both full-time in real estate.

The Fullers invited us to Houston to work with them in Texas. We did some research and found out Texas was a non-judicial state. That means foreclosures happen in less than thirty days, in most cases.

We sold everything we had in Albuquerque, which we called "the Land of Entrapment," a play on the state's real nickname, Land of Enchantment, packed up the Mercury Tracer Grandpa had bought for me, and moved to Texas. My dream of leaving the drug-infested town I knew so well finally became a reality. We were so proud of ourselves, but we were just beginning.

God was good to us. We believed moving to Texas was a part of His plan for us. We'd saved enough money to get by on until we got our Texas business up and running. It was scary, I won't lie. We had no family in Texas. But we had faith that God would watch over us, protect us, and guide us. And He did.

We followed the Fullers around for a while, learning everything we could from them. They had a booth at the Learning Annex in Dallas where they taught people how to work pre-foreclosures. We helped them with that. Charles had ten or twelve students at a time. They would find the deals. The Fullers would structure them and split the profits down the middle with his students.

Initially, the Fullers gave us a place to stay. They had a rental house about ten doors down from where they lived. Charles gave us the key to the house and we paid him rent until we could purchase a home of our own. A year later, we found one.

The passion for real estate grew in our hearts. Eventually, we worked up to a hundred and fifty houses a week. We got up in the morning, worked up our routes, packed our lunches, and hit the streets. Some days, we were out all day and night. We'd get home around 8 p.m. on a short day. And our philosophy was, whether it was five minutes or five hours, if you met a homeowner headed toward foreclosure, you were there until they signed on the dotted line. .

We had just moved to Texas at that point and didn't know the market very well. We were a little intimidated but driven. Shawn knocked on our first door and a huge guy, broad-shouldered and tall answered. Since I'm the bubbly non-threatening one, I'm the one who does the talking. Most people don't get mad, but this guy's face changed as soon as I started talking. He looked like he wanted to punch me.

"You have the audacity to knock on my door?" He slammed the glass storm door so hard it rattled. I thought the glass was going to break. Through the glass I could see his face, red with anger.

Shawn and I were known to be in people's homes as early as eight o'clock in the morning.

Like on one occasion, when we knocked on a door and a man in a T-shirt answered. He was holding a beer, Milwaukee's Best, in one hand.

"Good morning, Mr.—" I looked at the list of homeowners on my foreclosure list—"Dixon. I'm Joni Wolfswinkel. This is my husband Shawn. We found you on a list of people going into foreclosure and wanted to know if you'd sell your house."

"Come on in," he said. "Let's have a beer and talk about it."

What do you do? We wanted to mirror his behavior so we accepted the offer. We stepped inside, and he gave us a beer. It was awful. But we pretended to drink it by putting the can to our lips and faking a sip.

The man's couch was infested with Texas-sized cockroaches, but we sat on it. It was terrifying to sit anywhere, but that's the only way people feel comfortable talking to you.

As we talked to this man about buying his house, I glanced at Shawn's beer sitting on the coffee table and saw a cockroach crawling on it. I wanted to scream and run. Then I saw a cockroach crawling on the man's beard. He swatted it off. The cockroach hit the floor and scurried out of the room.

We were in his living room for two hours before closing the deal.

Over the ten years we knocked on doors, we had some crazy stuff happen. On another memorable occasion, Shawn and I were in for a real shock. Shawn knocked on the door and a lady answered. When I told her what we were there for, she said, "I know I need to sell, but I'm not ready. Can you come back tomorrow?"

We left and went back the next day. We'd already built rapport with her even though she wasn't ready to sell. She invited us into her house, so at least we were making progress.

So we thought.

It started with small talk. You have to get them to feel comfortable with you, so this part of the process can go quickly or it could take several hours. You have to patient. We plopped ourselves on our couch and chewed the fat. Innocent little chatter.

As we talked, we tried to encourage her to get through the process, sell her house, and save her credit. I told her when the sale date was going to be, it was coming up quickly, and stressed that time was of essence. She still wasn't ready.

She understood the urgency, but she was holding back. Shawn and I prepared the paperwork and went back a week later. She wanted to know what she could do with her belongings. She did have a lot of furniture.

I asked her if she had a place to go, any family or friends that could help. The way Shawn figured the math, she was going to squeeze about five thousand dollars out of her home's equity. I said, "You can use that money to find a place to live and start a new life."

Still, she wasn't ready. She had an uncle who had offered to let her stay at his house. I told her that was her best option. We even offered to help her move.

Just when we thought she was going to do it, she halted the process. We'd already drawn up the purchase agreement. All she had to do was sign and move out. We wouldn't give her any money until she did. That's the incentive to leave. But she balked.

One day, I went back by myself to see if I could talk her into it. Shawn was sick and encouraged me to go alone. So I did.

When the woman opened the door, she was very friendly. So friendly it was creepy. Then she asked me to come back the next day. I told Shawn he was going to have to go with me because I was freaked out.

When Shawn's health improved, we went back to the woman's house together. She flirted. She turned and walked down the hall. Curiously, we followed. When she reached her bedroom, she sat on the bed while Shawn and I planted ourselves at the door. She sat down, patted the bed with her hand, and said, "I want to *move* before I move."

"Oh my God," I gasped.

Shawn whispered in my ear, jokingly. "Take one for the team." But when she hiked her leg up and showed us some skin, Shawn gasped. "We really need to get this going so you can start your new life," he said.

Eventually, we got her to move. We had to rent a huge U-Haul truck and help her move all of her stuff to her uncle's house. It took a long time, but it was worth it in the end.

I became a hustler, a fearless tigress, willing to do about anything to get a real estate deal—except a threesome.

Another time, we got caught up in an ice storm. In Texas!

It didn't seem like a big deal at the time. I mean, it was just a little rain turning into ice. Or so I thought, until they shut the city down. We were in Houston. If you know Texas, it doesn't get many ice storms, but this particular one was one of the biggest the state had ever seen. We didn't know it at the time.

A woman had called to sell us her house in Round Rock, just north of Austin. When we looked at the Google photos, it looked like the house was built in the 1980s. In other words, it was outdated and needed a facelift.

As I spoke to the homeowner, she painted the worst picture of the property she could. I got the feeling she didn't really want to sell it. The subdivision this house was located in was located across the street from Dell, the computer manufacturer. In other words, it was in a decent neighborhood.

But her son, a developer, had told her the property was only good for its land value. He had told her the house should be leveled to the ground.

Hmmmm, I thought. *It must be a pretty crappy house.*

The land value was maybe $25,000. I figured we should go look at it. But I wasn't willing to write a check for $25,000 on a house that might be falling apart. So we drove three hours during an ice storm, from Houston to Austin, to look at her property.

I couldn't believe my eyes. We hit the jackpot!

All that house needed was some tender love and care. I pulled out my checkbook and hastily wrote a check for $25,000. I wrote it so fast it was barely readable.

The rehab costs were about $30,000. We sold it for $150,000 a few months later. It was the biggest deal we ever put together.

People thought we were crazy leaving the city in the middle of an ice storm, but it paid off. We could have easily told ourselves the weather was bad and we wouldn't be buying this house today. But we lived for that kind of stuff. We're not fair weather real estate investors.

On another occasion, we knocked on a door and someone from the master bedroom yelled out the window, "Who is it?" We told him. He invited us into his house and, boy, did he have big balls, we thought. Or maybe he was an idiot. We didn't know. But we walked right into a huge pile of beer cans in the living room. We couldn't see the floors, there were so many cans. And mice everywhere.

As we walked into the master bedroom, the gentleman, a man named John, lay in bed waiting for us. Depressed, he didn't want to get out of bed. His wife had passed away a few months earlier and all he wanted to do was drink.

It's a sad story, but his nephew lived across the street. From time to time, he would walk across the street to deliver his uncle's beer to him and take his money. All his uncle was to him was a paycheck.

The younger man was using his uncle for his house, his car, and his money.

John looked like death. Ants crawled all over him. He had ant bites from head to toe and was more pale than his bedsheets. He looked like he was about to die. He clearly needed medical attention.

Thank God we knocked on his door.

We could have called an ambulance, but we didn't. We put him in our car and drove him to the nearest VA hospital. He didn't have any family we could call, so we became his point of contact. He was so bad off the nurses couldn't get a pulse on him. They ran him into the emergency room immediately. He hadn't eaten in who knows how long and was severely dehydrated. The nurses told us if we didn't show up when we did, he would have died.

Over time, we grew apart from the Fullers. We started to notice Charles using us to find deals so that he wouldn't have to work any more. He was getting older, and more comfortable. Shawn and I was doing all the work—finding the deals, doing the rehab work, and selling the houses—while the Fullers sat by their pool enjoying themselves.

"You know what?" Shawn said one day. "We're in a position to do this on our own now." We made the decision to part ways.

When that partnership dissolved, we decided to offer the same type of joint-venture partnership to others that the Fullers had once offered us. We traveled around the country setting up partnerships. We had arrangements in Atlanta, Austin, Dallas, and a few cities in Florida. Our partners would find the deals and Shawn and I would fund them. It was a big win-win.

There were times when I questioned our commitment to real estate. *Why are we doing this*? I wondered. *Who could be crazy enough to live this life*? And then, around 2008, the market turned. The financial crisis hit and the real estate market changed. Retailing became difficult and properties sat longer on the market.

I told Shawn that we needed something more stable. Some months, you'd see a fifty thousand dollar paycheck, then there'd be months where you couldn't make a sale. So, we shifted our focus to property management.

At first, we thought it would be a nice supplement to our income. Then other investors started approaching us to help them.

Then they'd ask us to help them rent the houses. And there were a bunch of investors asking us to do that. That's when we came up with the turnkey model.

Shawn said, Let's try it and see if it works.

We were members of Houston's real estate investor club, so we purchased a vendor booth and got our first investor sign up.

We knew nothing about property management. We didn't know how to do an owner's statement. We started out with QuickBooks and spreadsheets. We just dove in and figured it out as we went. We needed to know what we were doing if we were to start managing other investors.

That's when we bought a Real Property Management franchise. We managed fifty doors our first year and ended up buying one hundred houses a year every year after that. Since 2010, we've managed thirteen hundred doors, total.

Shawn and I worked so hard and accomplished so much, but we were not finished. Every time we reached a goal, we raised the bar higher.

I love a challenge. I loved working hard, and still do, for something of value. I couldn't stop.

Choice Points:

- Hard work builds character - There's always something shiny to get your attention, but Shawn and I chose to get up every morning and treat our business like a job. It taught us discipline. We learned to focus our time and resources toward a goal. We also learned to ignore our critics. Plenty of people will doubt you, like they did me, but there is joy in proving them wrong. Quitting is easy. Giving up is easy. But easy doesn't build character, which is far more important than success.

- Hard work gets results - Hard work accomplishes something. So many times, I've learned something through the process. Have I make mistakes? Absolutely. In fact, I didn't know a damn thing about leadership. I never finished college. I went straight to building a business. Whether you're building a business or performing community service, hard work achieves results. Laziness wastes time and resources.

- Hard work creates opportunities - I cannot imagine getting where I am today without dedication and hard work. All those late nights knocking on doors, rehabbing properties, and traveling from state to state. The lazy complain about their lack of luck, but hard work opens doors. People who work hard create opportunities. Hard work is an opportunity magnet. Hard workers create their own luck.

THE CHOICE IS YOURS: CARE FOR YOURSELF

"Self-Care is not selfish, you cannot serve from an empty vessel."
— Eleanor Brown

If you've never had New Mexican food, you're missing out. It's a type of cuisine centered on the culture of New Mexico, formed out of the fusion of Mexican culinary practices, Pueblo cooking, and Hispano, an ethnic group native to New Mexico. The most defining ingredient is a chile pepper indigenous to New Mexico. I learned to master this type of cooking by watching my mother and mother-in-law.

When we first got married, Shawn and I craved New Mexican food. We particularly loved our moms' recipes. My mom was known for her red chile enchiladas and I learned how to make. We ate them twice a week. We'd eat chile peppers with eggs in the morning, and with our hamburgers at dinner time. We had this dish we called tortilla burgers, really popular in New Mexico, which consisted of flour tortillas wrapped around a hamburger and smothered with green chili sauce. We ate like that once or twice a week. With all the carbs, I gained thirty pounds right after marriage.

I have a hard time now believing it was truly me. It was as if someone had blown up a photo and enlarged every area of my body. When I look back, that extra thirty pounds is the evidence that I didn't respect my body. I didn't care what foods I put into it. I drank soda like it was going out of style. I actually avoided drinking water.

In high school, while active in sports, I was able to burn off the calories. But once Shawn and I were married, all we did was work and eat. I felt disgusting. Not pretty anymore.

I couldn't get into a swimsuit, and I didn't feel comfortable being around others wearing a swimsuit. I wore baggy clothes because I didn't want anyone to see me in bikini. And when Shawn and I were intimate, we'd turn off the lights because I was self-conscious about my appearance.

Unhappy with my body, I fell into a deep depression. I wanted to eat myself out of it.

Then I had children.

After birthing Lucas, I lost all self-confidence because I had gained more than sixty pounds. That was more than half my normal body weight. I was already feeling bad about myself and allowed my mind to feed me nonstop negativity.

With plenty of time on my hands, all I could do was sit, think, and talk to myself.

You're fat.

You're ugly.

You can't do that.

There were certain tasks I couldn't do because they had to be performed at the office. Shawn had to hire someone to help him with those things, which made me feel unworthy as a business partner. Plus, there were things around the house I couldn't do, which made me feel unworthy as a spouse. I was so hard on myself, which led to a further loss of confidence in myself.

I'm not the stay-at-home mom type. I'd go crazy if I had to stay at home all day and do nothing.

At one point, I was on bed rest because I had entered premature labor. I had been used to going to the office every day. I had a very active lifestyle. Then suddenly, I was stuck at home. It shattered my identity. Depression took over. I found out, if you're not prepared for it, pregnancy can take a real toll on you mentally.

All I wanted to do was eat, and it just got worse. I'd eat anything and everything that was set in front of me. Cake, brownies, cookies, any kind of sweets. And Coca-Cola. Boy, did I love drinking Coca-Cola.

If I'd had the mental strength at the time, I'd have read a book or listened to a podcast. I'd have found some way to motivate myself out of the mental funk I allowed myself to drift into. But I didn't. Instead, I ate, and ate, ate. And complained. And then complained some more.

Shawn got tired of it.

"Do something about it," he'd say. He wanted me to quit complaining. After all, I had a choice to eat or not eat. Or, as he'd say, "*What* you eat." He suggested I drink more water instead of Coca-Cola and eat healthy foods instead of snacks all the time.

Of course, he was right. (It was during this time that I started journaling. For some helpful tips on journaling for self-awareness, see Appendix 5.)

I knew I had to take control of my eating habits. I was afraid that Shawn wasn't going to think I was pretty, or that he wouldn't want to have sex with me. I mean, that was my fear talking. It wasn't reality. I finally realized I needed to do something about my body weight, so I joined the Quick Weight Loss Center in Houston.

I joined the program not long after Lucas was born and kept it up long after Mila was born. If you had asked my family, they'd have said I was crazy. They didn't understand. To them, the only people who should join a weight-loss program are people over two hundred pounds. Because most of them are overweight, their point of reference is different. Since I wasn't bigger than they are, in their minds, I couldn't be overweight. Nevertheless, I felt I needed to lose thirty pounds, or more. That drove me to seeking professional help.

I knew what I had been doing wasn't working. In my mind, I could transfer my success in real estate to success at losing weight. That's why I dedicated myself to a weight-loss program. Once a day, I'd drive to the weight-loss center and weigh in. That was the first thing I did every day.

My nutritionist, Lisa, made me a meal plan each week. I drank eighty ounces of water a day, no alcohol.

Lisa insisted that I consume no alcohol or soda throughout the program. Come on, no soda? No alcohol? How was I ever going to accomplish this? I wondered.

But I did it. Each day, I'd go to the weight-loss center with their weight-loss tracker and write down what my weight was. I'd also catalog the foods I ate. I'd record whatever I had for breakfast, lunch, dinner, and snacks. And they would checkmark each food item on a list to be sure I was eating all the right foods. If I substituted a chocolate chip cookie for one of their cookies, they'd gig me for that. It was their way of holding me accountable, and it worked.

Their list of foods was bland, too. No salt, no flavorings, no spices. Nothing like that. We ate chicken, turkey, and fish. A lot of protein, red meat only once or twice a week. And we also ate a lot of vegetables. It was usually steamed veggies or a salad, and one or two starches each day.

Every time I went to the nutritionist's office, I weighed a few pounds less. And I got more excited. It motivated me to continue my journey, to keep working the plan. While the food was bland, I was not going to back down.

Before I knew it, ninety days had passed and I'd lost thirty pounds. Members of my family made comments like, "That has to be unhealthy. How can a person lose that much weight in such a short period of time?"

It was hard, but I formed new eating habits.

I became disciplined in what I ate for breakfast, lunch, and dinner. I consumed a lot of protein, but not much sugar. And I pushed that down to Lucas and Mila, so they'd eat right.

Before joining the weight-loss program, we'd eat a lot of cheeseburgers, Philly cheesesteaks, and that kind of thing. It was comfort food. If I had a bad day, a cheeseburger could solve it. Not any more.

Instead, I went to the gym and worked out. Or I'd go for a walk or a bike ride.

I felt good about myself. Because I felt good about myself, I was happier. I felt beautiful again. And I felt like I accomplished more at work too. But the crown jewel of rewards was the sex Shawn and I had afterwards.

I was so grateful about what I had learned about eating, I turned that new knowledge into a lifestyle.

After I lost all that weight, Shawn and I went out to celebrate. We went to the Hibachi Grill where we could eat fried rice, steak, shrimp, everything I had denied myself for weeks. I got so sick I lay in bed for three days. Despite not liking it, I went back to the meal plan.

The mental shift helped me bounce back. When I had Lucas, I gained sixty pounds. With Mila, it was forty pounds. Yes, I gained a lot of weight and made extra-big babies. I blame it on Shawn. He came into the world as a big baby with a huge head.

Lucas was born a month early and weighed just under nine pounds. Mila went full term, but she weighed eight pounds. Both times, pregnancy was tough on me. Not only did I gain a tremendous amount of weight, but I had complications.

With Lucas, I went into labor prematurely two months before the due date.

The day before I went into labor, Shawn and I were at the NCAA Final Four tournament in Houston. Shawn's parents were UCLA fans, so we went to see them play.

It sounded great at the time, until I had to walk a mile to get from the parking lot to the stadium. Any other pregnant woman would have requested to be dropped off at the stadium entrance, if she went at all. Not me.

When I got to the stadium, I was dying. And then there was a flight of stairs. There I was, waddling around the basketball stadium, about to burst, overweight, and hot as hell. But I never complained. I didn't want to miss the action. Shawn and I were huge fans of sporting events. We weren't going to miss it. If I was nine months pregnant, I'd have stayed home, but seven months? In my mind, it was a piece of cake.

I believe attending that game, and the amount of walking it put me through, triggered me into labor. I was in the hospital for bed rest for almost two weeks.

I was scheduled to have my baby shower that day. We had invited close to one hundred fifty people.

I got up that morning and drove to the nail salon to get a pedicure. When I walked out of the nail salon, I felt something and thought, *This doesn't feel right.* So I went back inside and headed to the bathroom. I was bleeding. Only ten minutes from the house, I went to the car and got behind the wheel. As I drove, I called Shawn to tell him I was bleeding.

When I got home, Shawn's mom was there. She had flown down from New Mexico for the baby shower. Right away, she told me we needed to get to the hospital. That the placenta could be detached. Shawn drove me while his mom and sister continued preparing for the baby shower.

When Shawn and I got to the hospital, they performed an ultrasound. Dr. Jenna Everson said, "You're not having a baby shower today. You're going into labor. "

Two months was too early. I'd have tried anything to keep Lucas cooking a little longer, but nature doesn't take orders.

The doctor wasn't about to let me go home either. She wanted to keep a close eye on me to make sure I didn't overdo it. After two weeks in the hospital, Dr. Everson sent me home for more bed rest. She added strict rules, essentially confining me to the bed and the bathroom.

I was devastated. I had already spent two weeks in the hospital. Now, I was going to spend the rest of my pregnancy on bed rest? I spiraled into depression again.

I did as much as I could while on bed rest. I may have been in bed, and I may have been resting, but it didn't mean I couldn't work. I answered emails, handled conference calls, and watched a lot of movies to keep my mind off the things I was not able to do.

Shawn did his best to keep me motivated. He read a lot of books and listened to podcasts. When he came across something he thought would benefit me, he would send it to me.

He tried hard to stay positive. And when he got home from work, he'd put everything to the side and focus on me.

I also watched a lot of Lifetime with my mom to pass the time. But I really wanted to work. I tried being productive. Shawn would send me market analyses on properties, and I'd perform them. I'd research properties and do computer work to take my mind off of bed rest. It was a struggle.

At this time, we were still flipping properties. We hadn't started the property management business yet. The stuff I would normally do, like designing homes to make them sellable, Shawn had to take care of them. And he didn't complain. He simply adjusted.

About a month before Lucas was due, my water broke. I was having this baby and there was nothing that could stop it. We had just moved into a new house in Cypress, Texas. The hospital, Memorial Hermann in The Woodlands, was an hour away. Still, Shawn, with Mom's help, put me in the car and took me to the hospital.

We hit every red light along the way, so the trip was twice as long as it should have been.

I thought I was going to die. Every time I felt a contraction, I screamed. "Hurry up!" I wanted him to drive like Paul Walker in the *Fast and Furious* movies.

We finally arrived at the hospital. Shawn, Mom, my mother-in-law, and me. It was Lucas time.

I asked for drugs the moment Mom wheeled me in. I wanted the epidural as soon as possible. I wasn't holding out for a natural childbirth. I wanted to be as *unnatural* as possible. The sooner the better. They were already late.

I couldn't imagine having Lucas without an epidural. And when push time came, it was unbelievably difficult trying to push him out. The harder I pushed, the more tired I got. The doctor, calm as a placid lake, would tell me, "Push harder." How could she be so calm? This was my big-headed baby coming into the world.

The moment came when Lucas's head crowned. His head was out, but his body was still inside me. He was stuck, and all I remember is the doctor calmly encouraging, "Push, Joni. I need you to push." She threatened to push Lucas's big head back in and perform a C-section.

There was no damn way Lucas's head was going back inside of me. I pushed as hard as I could, and prayed. The doctor called for back up.

Back up? Was this a police procedural? I had no clue what was going on. All drugged up and dying from the pain of Lucas's oversized hat rack, all I remember was five nurses and a few doctors preparing for a worst-case scenario. I wanted it to end.

Shawn looked like a ghost, and Mom was huddled in a corner crying her heart out. Shawn paced back and forth like the general manager of a baseball team losing the World Series. This was the man who fainted when I got my belly button pierced. He didn't know what to do.

Shawn's mother, the OB-GYN, was the only member of the family staying calm. She stood by my side, acting as my coach. "One last big push," she said. I gave it everything I had, pushed as hard as I could. I was not giving up. The doctor reached in and grabbed Lucas as I grunted and pushed with all my might. Finally, he popped out, big head and all.

He was huge. A month early and just an ounce shy of nine pounds.

Had I gone full term, he could have been eleven pounds. How could a newborn baby be that big? Could the doctor have miscalculated my due date? That was my first thought, but Lucas showed signs of being premature. His ears were not fully developed.

Lucas gave me a fourth degree vaginal tear, and my stomach was stretched beyond belief. I worked hard to get back to where I was before, but my body would never get back to normal without plastic surgery. I knew it. Even with plastic surgery, it was never going to be the same.

Still, I worked hard to take care of myself. I'd eat right, breast feed defiantly, and exercise to shed off the weight. I knew I wasn't going to be the same, but I'd do anything to feel better about myself.

I was okay not being perfect as long as I was perfect for Shawn. That's all that mattered to me.

For awhile, I thought Lucas would be my one and only baby. I couldn't imagine going through that again. But Shawn and I enjoyed having a baby in the house. Lucas talked about having a brother or sister, so we talked about having another baby. At one point, we thought about adopting. Not right away, of course, but we couldn't imagine Lucas being the only child. Three years later, I was pregnant with Mila.

Pregnancy with Mila was different. I had morning sickness, but it wasn't as bad as with Lucas. I didn't gain as much weight with Mila, which was the best part. And she was a scheduled C-Section. Dr.

Everson was not about to let me have this baby the natural way. She was afraid Mila would get stuck the way Lucas did.

When time came to have Mila, all went well in the delivery room and I was mom to a precious little girl. I'd like to say that everything went perfectly, but how often does anything go perfectly? It seemed like I had to work hard for everything in life.

Once again, the delivery came with complications.

After delivery, I held Mila in my arms with motherly love. Luckily, Shawn was at the hospital. I told him I wasn't feeling well. I felt light-headed. In fact, I felt like passing out, so I handed him the baby. And fainted.

Shawn, freaking out, called for the doctor. They rushed me to the emergency room.

There had to be something wrong. What caused me to pass out? After a few tests, they discovered I had lost a lot of blood due to a blood vessel in my stomach bursting. I lost so much blood I was going to need a transfusion.

I couldn't believe it. Didn't I have enough trauma with the first pregnancy? Mila was going to be the last baby, for sure. My poor body wasn't doing so well carrying babies.

After the blood transfusion, I felt better. I was able to go home. With a little discipline, I was able to bounce back to my pre-pregnancy weight, although it took ninety days.

I went back to the habits I learned from the Quick Weight Loss Center. I started eating bland foods again with a few mini-snacks throughout the day, and drinking a lot of water. I also exercised more. Mentally, I regained my strength and discipline. I was determined to overcome.

Shawn and his mom tried to get me to slow down. The doctors told me to wait four to six weeks before going back to my normal routine, but I couldn't wait. I was at it the next week. Lucas was in day care, but Mila wasn't old enough yet. She had to be at least three months old before day care would take her, so I took her to the office with me and set up a play pen for her. When she needed to be fed, I'd shut the door to my office and breastfeed her, then I'd go back to my work.

I was trying to find my balance.

Through it all, I kept the weight-loss regimen a regular part of my routine. And I've managed to keep the extra weight off ever since. (For some tips on self-care, see Appendix 7.)

Choice Points:

- Push - It doesn't matter if it's day-to-day work, birthing a child, or following a diet plan, if you treat it seriously and discipline yourself to do what is necessary, you will succeed. Anything I put my mind to, I give it one hundred ten percent. There are obstacles in every aspect of our lives. The winners push.

- Take care of yourself first - On airplanes, they tell you put your own oxygen mask on first before you put one on your child. The reason is, if you go unconscious before you get your child's mask on, your child is doomed. Time is precious. Make every moment count and make yourself your top priority. You can't be effective as mom, wife, or entrepreneur if you're not healthy. Put first things first and take care of yourself.

- Say "no" to others and "yes" to self-care- Learning to say "no" is really hard. Many of us feel obligated to say "yes" when someone asks for our time and energy. However, if you're already stressed or overworked, saying "yes" to loved ones or coworkers can lead to burnout, anxiety, and irritability. It may take a little practice, but once you learn to politely say "no," you'll feel more self-confident and have time to care for yourself.

THE CHOICE IS YOURS: MAKE YOUR FAMILY A PRIORITY

"You define what is important to you by what you dictate your time to." — Monica Bakhla

Lucas and Mila are now ten and six years old, respectively. They know they have hard-working parents. They are accustomed to our work schedules and daily routines and are as adaptable as we are. We are grooming them for their own success stories.

When Lucas was born, Shawn and I didn't know what to do. I was a new parent with a budding career. How was I going to care for a child *and* help my husband run the business? It was a problem in need of a solution, and we found it. But that doesn't mean there weren't challenges.

Every parent has challenges. Every business owner has them too. Sometimes, challenges as a parent and a business owner collide. Like forgetting to pack your child's lunch for school. Or missing a really important office meeting. Then there's forgetting your child's school event, or a lunch date with your daughter.

I've done each of these things. And felt horrible about each one. It's easy to feel like the worst mom in the world. To feel pulled between our roles and priorities.

We all make mistakes. As a working mom, there are days when we run around a hundred miles an hour trying to make ends meet. When we get to moving that fast, it's easy to let go of one of those ends.

Life is about choices. I had to learn to make some difficult ones. We all do. Or we can choose to listen to the demons as they tell us we're not worthy or not good enough for success, not good enough to be good parents, etc.

I chose to believe that I was able to drive a business, could be a good wife to Shawn, and be a good mother to our children. There's power in choosing the messages we're going to believe.

Is it easy? Hell no. Every day, we are thrown a collection of curve balls. How we react to those curve balls dictates the outcome of our lives. We may not hit all of them, but with the right attitude, the odds are in our favor that we'll hit a few.

Some people freeze. Or analyze it and forget to swing the bat. They act like the pitch is unhittable. Let the negative voices around them and inside their heads convince them they can't win. Sabotage themselves with negative self-talk instead of filling their minds with positive affirmations.

In short, they hand the victory over to their demons.

When Lucas and Mila were a few months old, Shawn and I put them in daycare. With a business to run and no family to help us, we did what we had to do. We had to manage the dual challenges of raising children and building a business. How could I put my children in daycare while I went to work, chasing my entrepreneurial dreams? I felt selfish. I felt like a terrible mom.

But that, you see, was my demons crafting a negative story in my head. Self-talk. And it's destructive.

Others were judging me, telling me I chose work over family. And I believed them. I allowed their criticisms to get inside my head and destroy my self-confidence. To this day, people still judge me. But I had to learn to put on thick skin and wear it like a pantsuit. Raising children as an entrepreneur was *my* choice. No one else has a right to judge that.

It wasn't easy making that choice either.

Why did I care so much about other people's opinions? Did it matter what they thought about my lifestyle choices? I let it matter for a while. The truth is, I was a people pleaser. I wanted to please people I didn't know or like. I spent *hours* worrying about what they thought of me. Why?

Worrying what others thought of me was the worst thing I could have done. It was ruining me. I constantly questioned myself. *Am I a good mother*? *Am I a good wife*? And the worst part is, I'd compare myself to other women, entertaining such thoughts as *I wish I was beautiful like* her, *I wish I could be a great wife and mom like* her, or *I wish I had a body like* hers. This self-talk was devastating me.

111

So how did I overcome it? By choice!

It started with choosing to believe in myself. Choosing to believe that nothing mattered as long as my family was taken care of and that I was happy living the life I wanted to live.

The moment I chose to change my mindset was the moment my life changed for the better. It was the moment I regained control of my life forever. It was the moment that led to true happiness and satisfaction. Because of this choice, my home was a happy home. My husband and children were happy, and so was I. And who cared what anyone else thought about it? They weren't paying our bills.

The demons have a boatload of lies.

I've been told things like, "You are successful because you married into success." I've also been told I'm not good enough for success. And here's one of my favorites: "You'll never amount to anything."

That's a total crock! Everyone is worth something.

I've had family members tell me I'm too pretty to be successful. They'd tell me no one would ever take me seriously.

I've also been told it's not possible to have both beauty and brains. I've been told I'm successful only because I inherited money. Considering my background, I have to laugh at that one.

Other lies the demons tell: I don't eat enough and that I'm going to get sick if I don't put meat on my bones; I shouldn't go out with friends on the weekends and leave my children with a baby sitter; I travel too much without my family,that I need to stay home more, thatit will have a negative effect on my children's mental health.

If people say these things to me now, it adds fuel to my fire. It energizes me. Motivates me.

Many people underestimate me based on my background. They judge me on the basis of my backstory. Or because I'm a woman. Until I accepted the fact that my life is mine to live, I struggled. I struggled emotionally, psychologically, spiritually, and financially. Until I changed my mindset, I couldn't beat the demons telling me that I couldn't be a successful career-minded woman and a wife and mother at the same time.

I'm not demonizing people here. Some of them are well-intentioned, but they're not living my life—or yours. The demons are the voices that well up inside ourselves, and others, who speak negativity without a purpose. The criticism isn't meant to build up, but tear down.

I used to listen to the voices, and I believed them. It wasn't until I changed my way of thinking that I became unstoppable. I felt at peace knowing I was doing the best I could. I improved my routine and got better at scheduling priorities, which created a balance between my spiritual life, my family life, my business life, my fitness life, and my social life. Once I believed I could create that balance, I became unstoppable. I felt like I had it all.

Until I changed my mindset , I'd wake up wondering how I was going to get through the day. Sound familiar?

I'd wake up at 4:30 a.m. to work out and hit the shower at 5:30. Then I'd wake my children at six o'clock to get them ready for school. I made the family breakfast and drove an hour round trip to drop the kids off at their respective schools. There was barely enough time to grab a cup of coffee on the way to work. I was exhausted by the time I arrived around 8:30 each morning.

That morning routine was followed by a hard day at work. The days were filled with unhappy clients, employees to manage, and little time for a lunch break. In the afternoon, I left the office at 5:15 to pick the kids up from school by six. When I got home, I made dinner, bathed the kids, helped them with homework, and put them to bed by 8:30. (In Appendix 6, I go into detail about my current daily routine. Feel free to flip back there for a glimpse into how I manage my life and time today.)

The next day, I got up and did it all over again.

Over time, I learned to embrace my morning time with my children, viewing it as quality relationship time.

I'd cry myself to sleep wondering how I was going to make it another day. Then the kids would get sick, but I still had to manage leading my work team, and the family on the home front. It wore me out.

Then I found the solution that changed my mindset.

One of the things I did was hire a nanny. I couldn't be in twenty places at once, so she helped me with things around the house and did some things for Lucas and Mila, which freed up my time to focus on the right things. When I go home, I focused on relating to my husband and children instead of doing chores. It made a big difference.

When the nanny gave her two week notice, I wondered what I was going to do. Shawn wanted to hire another nanny, but I decided to go another route.

"What if that person quits?" I said. "Then we'll be stuck in the same position."

So that's when I put Lucas in daycare. When Mila was old enough, she went to daycare. I was criticized for it, but it's my life and my family. We had to do what was best for us.

Choice Points:

- You are not your mistakes - Mistakes are a part of life. We all make them. But don't let the mistakes of the past set you in a negative loop pattern. Forgive yourself, forgive others, and get back on the horse. Learn from your mistakes and turn them into future successes.

- Don't listen to criticism - You and your family deserve your own lives. Others will criticize you for the choices you make, but don't listen. You must do what is best for you and your family. That's your business. Let others mind theirs.

- Develop a routine - Everything you do determines your success. How you raise your children, whether you put them in daycare, how much time you spend on extra-curricular activities, and even your morning routine all contribute to your success. Set your priorities in order so that the important things aren't missed.

- Schedule family time - Often, the busyness of life takes over. This is why purposefully scheduling family time is necessary. One of the easiest ways to do this is to designate a weekly family or date night. During this time, the family is focused on being together.

- Change your mindset - The key to overcoming your challenges is to stay positive. Quit feeling sorry for yourself. You, too, will find success and happiness through the journey if you focus on the right things.

- It starts with you! - You are an essential element to your family's planned time together. You need to be there, and you need to be engaged. The laundry can wait another thirty minutes. You can clean the kitchen after the kids have gone to sleep. Toys can be picked up tomorrow. You can DVR that show. Facebook will be there after you finish a game of Life or Uno. You can answer messages on your phone just before going to bed or first thing in the morning. Remember, YOU are modeling behaviors for your little ones.

THE CHOICE IS YOURS: LIVE WITH NO REGRETS

"You can control your own life, your own will is extremely powerful." — JK Rowling

Shawn and I started our walk with faith in 2003 while still in New Mexico. There was a non-denominational church in Albuquerque called Hoffmantown West. When we moved to Texas several years later, we wanted a similar church so we searched for one we could involve ourselves in and that would keep us motivated. It didn't take long.

We visited three or four churches in the The Woodlands and found a large church we liked called Fellowship of the Woodlands. It was a young church with small groups and a great band. The crowd was younger, so it fit us. We met people who would become very good friends.

Being surrounded by like-minded people who joined us in prayer made all the difference in the world. Prayer became a regular part of our routine. We prayed in the mornings, in the evenings, at meal time, before we went to bed at night, and with our small group. This became very important to Lucas and Mila because they both attended Christian private schools and prayer was a big part of their education. Prayer has made a big difference in how my family deals with the struggles of life.

I've gone through traumatic experiences, but God was always there. He is the one who bailed me out of every awful situation. From the time Shawn and I met until today, everything we did, every obstacle we overcame, every ounce of success, we attribute it all to God working in our lives.

Our big God moment happened when Shawn and I moved to Texas. Before that, I lived in fear of everything. But Shawn and I made the move and gave it all to God, trusting Him for the results. Everything worked out fine for us in the end.

When we put our house in New Mexico on the market, it sold in five days. From that time on, things just fell in place as God ordained it. Our transition from there to moving into Shawn's parents' house, and then relocating to Texas, all went smoothly.

Going through the experiences I went through as a child was God's way of strengthening me. He challenged me and helped me overcome those challenges so that I can share my life with others and be an encouragement. Even today, He continues to challenge and strengthen me. I believe He's growing me for something even bigger.

It also makes me a better person. Trusting God has made me think more deeply about life and how fleeting it is. I learned how to forgive, and I'm more at peace.

When I lost Joey, my one and only brother, I was thirty-one years old. Losing someone that close gave me a new perspective in life. I had done everything I could to help him. Joey's drug addiction was out of my control, but it wasn't out of God's. Still, for a long time, I blamed myself for his death. That is, until I learned to give it to God.

I felt guilty after his death because I felt like I didn't do enough to save him from the addiction that he fought. In hindsight, I was in denial about the severity of his condition. It wasn't until he asked to move in with Shawn and me that I realized Joey had a real problem.

Where we lived, there was a park nearby. I'd wake up and walk to the park, sit at a picnic table, and cry my eyes out. I didn't want Shawn to see the tears. The park became my sanctuary, a place to hide my sorrow. *Why won't you change him?* I'd ask. Emotionally, I was shaking my fist at God.

A few weeks later, Joey was living with us, a jobless, total wreck. When Shawn and I started to argue about it, that was the tipping point.

Maybe I could have, and should have, done more to help Joey, but, at the end of the day, I had to choose what was right for my family. I had a husband, and children.

While it was a tough choice, I had to move forward with my life. That was the only sensible thing to do. The devil wants me to think,

I',m crazy. I chose myr relationship with Shawn over my relationship with Joey, my own blood." Some of you may be thinking that too.

Life is messy. I knew the life I wanted, and there's only so much you can do for someone hell-bent on self-destruction. I made a choice. For good or ill. I had to live with it.

Believe me, I've lived with it.

Years later, after we moved to Texas, Mom would call me whenever she was dealing with Joey and his addiction. She vented, and complained. I listened.

"Mom, he's going to do what he wants to do," I told her. "Let him go."

I regretted it. I wondered if I had done enough for Joey. Could I have saved him? Probably not, but the demons in my head wanted me to believe I hadn't done enough. It made me angry. I got angry at Mom, angry at Joseph, and angry at the world. It was guilt and fear.

One day, Joey and Mom had a falling out. He had moved to Roswell to be close to our father. My aunt called Mom and told her that Joey had fainted in Walmart. They rushed him to the hospital.

Initially, they thought something was wrong with his heart, so they recommended that he see a specialist. After three or four days in the hospital, he started going through withdrawals. He couldn't handle it, so he got up and left the hospital. Mom and my aunt were there at the time.

A couple of weeks later, Joey called me. "Joni, I'm not doing well," he said. "I'm going to die."

"No you're not," I was crying. "It will be okay." I never heard from him again.

Later that day, they airlifted him from Roswell to Albuquerque. I told Shawn I was going to Albuquerque even though I wasn't ready to accept that Joey was dying. I didn't want to believe it.

Before leaving, I needed to ease my mind, so I went home and crawled into bed. Over night, while sleeping, my stepfather called. "Joni, Joey had a cardiac arrest."

After Joey died, I felt relieved. The guilt and fear disappeared. I thought, *Nothing else can happen to him now.* His funeral service was in Santa Fe. He looked so heavy and blown up. I could barely recognize him, he was so swollen from the fluids they pumped into him.

Three years later, Joseph overdosed. That was before I chose to fight my demons. Now I'm left with some big unknowns.

I had so many questions for him, but they won't be answered now. I wanted to tell him I forgive him for all the pain he caused. Now I'll never have the chance.

About a year after Joseph's passing, I reached out to his parents, which opened the door to a beautiful relationship. I took Shawn, Lucas, and Mila to visit them at Christmas that year. It was awkward since I hadn't seen them in over twenty years. My grandparents were aging and I didn't want to have the same regrets that I have with my father. I felt it was important to meet with them.

We had great conversations. They mostly talked about Joey, which has always been typical on both sides of my family. They didn't talk much about Joseph. Nevertheless, it was great getting to know them.

More importantly, it was great spending time with my first cousins. I had always wanted cousins. But because I was shut off from that side of the family, I felt deprived. There are four cousins I had never met before: Kazira, Aysia, Camra, and Jared. Bonding with them became, in a way, its own therapy. I found out they had some of the same feelings as me.

Jared said he felt cheated.

Aysia didn't know who to be angry with, but she felt deprived of experiencing a normal human privilege.

There was selfishness on both sides of the family. Mom hated my father for what he did to her. I don't blame her one bit, from the beatings she took, dealing with his drug addiction, and abandoning us, but was it the rest of the family's fault?

I still have a way to go and want to know so much more about the family I've missed.

Joseph's mother is a tough egg to crack. She has some bitterness, and anger, towards me. I'm not quite sure why she feels like the victim. She didn't make much of an effort to see me over the last twenty years. I chose to be the better person and forgive.

Despite this big gaping hole, there is a bright side. My cousins.

They have open doors and open arms. They call me and invite me to places. When I visit them in Santa Fe we'll sit down for breakfast or lunch together. After so many years without a relationship, we can now focus on being the family we didn't have.

You can be a better person. Life may not go as you planned, but at the end of the day, you will not have regrets. You can live a happier life by being grateful for the things you do have. Joey didn't try to teach me this lesson, but he taught me to live life to its fullest. And that's another choice we all make. We can shrink from the challenge or embrace it. We can live life to the fullest or hold back. Joey chose to shrink from the challenge. I chose to embrace it. What will you choose? (Once again, flip back to Appendix 3 to read my thoughts on living life to the fullest.)

Choice Points:

- Live every moment like it's your last - All of us have an end date, but we don't know when it is. Live like to the fullest and make the most of every minute.

- Have no regrets - You'll have tough choices. Think them through carefully and make the best one for you and your loved ones. You can't save anyone hell-bent on self-destruction. Sometimes, you can't help but watch a train wreck. Unless you're driving the train, don't blame yourself. You can't make someone else's decisions for them.

- Take risks- Staying within your comfort zone may be safe, but it is impossible to achieve greatness by living cautiously.

- Take life less seriously- Life is far too short to be spent worrying about things that are beyond our control. Allow fun to be a part of your life each day. Being mindful and open to the good that is present in all situations can help us not take life seriously and is a key ingredient to having enjoying life.

- Turn failures into stepping stones - Don't quit when you perceive you have failed. Instead, learn from the experience and use it to grow yourself.

- Practice Forgiveness - We all have hurts. How we deal with those hurts is up to us. Some people stay stuck in bitterness their entire lives. They never move beyond the pain. By choosing to forgive, we release ourselves from the grip of resentment and move forward in our lives.

THE CHOICE IS YOURS: BE SUCCESSFUL

"She knows the power of her mind and so programmed it for success." — Carrie Greer

Have you ever been told how lucky you are? Maybe it's about having a certain job. Or being in a certain relationship. Maybe they've told you that you're lucky to be pretty, have a great family, or because you have great health.

Well, I don't believe luck has much to do with it.

I've been told I'm lucky to be married to a great guy. I believe I am. But not for the reasons people imply.

I've been told I'm lucky to have the ability to work with my husband. Most couples can't fathom working together, but Shawn and I have built a business together. This "luck," as they call it, is simply envy.

As I write this, many people are social distancing due to the coronavirus pandemic, and they're finding that being cooped up in their homes with their spouses for an extended period of time is frustrating. It's causing marriage problems for some of them. Not for Shawn and me.

Other things I'm "lucky" to have: a "good head on your shoulders." To not be overweight. To have well-behaved children.

The big one is this: "You're so lucky to have the life you have, being married to Shawn."

That lie is based on Shawn being the son of a successful doctor and me coming from the other side of the tracks. I didn't have a lot of money growing up. My father and brother were drug addicts. Dysfunction ran through my family like an Olympic sprinter on steroids. So I was "lucky" Shawn came along to rescue me from all of that.

To hear some of these people tell it—some are family—Shawn is the reason for my success. They praise him to the point that I don't get any credit at all.

Let me say this, my friends: Success is no accident!

I'm extremely blessed to have the husband that I have. Shawn is a great guy. We love each other. We have two beautiful children together. We've managed to build two successful businesses together. You could say we have four "babies."

I'm very blessed to have a man who meets all of my needs. *And* I've made choices along the way that have contributed to our success. Shawn and I are a team. We're partners in business and in life. Our success was achieved together.

It wasn't luck that got me where I am today. It wasn't luck that made me fit and healthy. And it isn't luck that makes my children listen to me when I talk. What is it?

Success is a choice. In fact, everything in life is a choice. Like other successful entrepreneurs, I chose the path to success. I choose to give one hundred percent to everything I do. I choose to live a lifestyle that makes me healthy. At the end of the day, it was hard work, sacrifice, and perseverance that brought me to where I am today.

The truth is, anyone can be successful. What's stopping *you*?

You are the only one stopping you from being successful. Stop telling yourself that awful story that you can't (fill in the blank), or that you're not built for (your dream). I know that you are.

But I'm not going to sugarcoat it for you. You may have to go through a series of failures before you experience success. I did. All great leaders do. But, like me, you can learn from your failures, pick yourself up again, and move up the rungs of the ladder to true success in life. As defined by you. It's all a matter of making the right choices.

In our household, for instance, the word "can't" is not allowed. I want my children to grow up believing they can do anything they put their minds to. Of course, there are going to be obstacles, even failures, but they can choose to get back up and go at it again. And so can you.

Regardless of your circumstances, you can choose success.

The first part of success is feeling good about yourself, inside and out. This will boost your self-esteem, and it will help build your confidence. As a woman and as a business leader.

What drives you? What gets you fired up and out of bed in the morning? You have to figure out what that one thing is that drives you. No one else can do it for you.

When I was younger, I had a burning drive to prove everyone wrong. Because of my health issues, as well as the family I was born into, nobody, and I mean *nobody*, had much faith in me. That drove me to prove everyone wrong. I was not born an entrepreneur. I was *bred* an entreprenuer. It was hard work—hustling and surrounding myself with winners—that got me to where I am today. This can be illustrated through the twists and turns I took while playing sports as a child.

In elementary school, Joey played baseball and basketball. I thought, *Okay, Mom loves that he's playing baseball and basketball, so maybe I should play those sports.*

In an attempt to earn Mom's approval, I played the same sports. Good thing, wrong reason.

In elementary school, I was the only girl on the basketball team. Then Joey joined the wrestling team, so I joined the wrestling team. Again, the training was good for my development, but I did it for the wrong reason.

I was pretty good at it too. When I tell my children I was a wrestler and placed first and second in most of my matches, they think it's hilarious. But they also think it's cool that their mama was a wrestler.

One day, Shawn found a picture of me wrestling another girl. He thought it was the cutest thing. When he wants to embarrass me, he breaks out this pathetic wrestling picture of me. Nevertheless, I think it's awesome to be able to share this moment with my children, to show them how determined I was as a child.

In middle school, I tried out for the volleyball and the track teams. In eighth grade, I was the most valuable player on the girls track team. At that moment, I impressed myself.

I wasn't the most talented athlete in school. I could name a handful of girls who were much more talented than me. The secret to my success, however, was hard work. I'm proud of the fact that I worked harder than anyone else at any endeavor.

I ran the 100- and 200-meter dashes, and relays. In eighth grade, we had ten meets throughout the year. I placed in every one of them, first or second.

All of this is to say, success comes through trials, errors, and failures. I've had my fair share of them, as well victories. You will too.

Have you ever heard the saying, "You are who you hang out with?"

To narrow it down more specifically, motivational speaker Jim Rohn said, "You are the average of the five people you spend the most time with."

Think about that for a second. If you want to be a millionaire, would you hang out with people who have no motivation in life, no job, and no goals? I know I wouldn't. I like to hang out with successful entrepreneurs. People who have the same ambitions, dreams, and goals that I have. These influences have factored into my success.

Maybe you're not sure what that looks like for you. Start by educating yourself. Read books, listen to podcasts, feed your mind with positivity. Soon, your drive will turn into passion. I now have a passion to share my journey with my children, with my staff, and with you.

I have learned not to put limits on myself. If I say I'm going to do something, then I will make it a point to get it done, no matter how uncomfortable it makes me.

One area where I have made that commitment to myself is in public speaking. When I'm about to speak in front of a group, I tend to freak out. My heart races and I forget what I want to say. It's embarrassing and, yes, I could easily tell myself that I'm not going to put myself in that situation again.

It would be easy to give up on public speaking altogether. If I did that, I'd only hurt myself. I'd be limiting *me*.

Instead, I push myself to do better. If I speak in front of people more often, I will get better at it. Soon, I won't have this awful feeling, and a fear of public speaking. At least, I'll have an effective way of managing fear so that it doesn't get the better of me.

When the real estate market crashed in 2008 and 2009, Shawn and I could have quit. We could have said, well, it looks like flipping houses isn't lucrative anymore, so let's find some other kind of business, something other than real estate, to get into. We had to adapt our business model to the current situation if we were going to survive.

So we pivoted.

That was the year we launched our property management company and, since then, our business has succeeded overall. There were some rocky times, but we've done well.

As I write this, the country is reeling from COVID-19. Some states have shut down government services and nonessential businesses. The economy is spiraling into an abyss. Schools have sent children home permanently and out-of-work parents are wondering what they're going to do to keep their out-of-school children occupied. I've heard people say that they're not teachers and can't home-school their children. It's only too hard if you let it be too hard. It's about adapting to the situation.

There's no time to be complacent. You can't allow yourself to be spoiled on the fat of the good times. Economies move in cycles. In fact, throughout American history, according to the Federal Reserve, there has been a recession one out of every five years. People in any business who succeed financially do so because they plan for the recessionary economies, instead of being freaked out by them. They're rarely taken by surprise, are flexible, and adapt to the forces which they cannot control.

I've put Lucas and Mila in time out for ten or fifteen minutes just for saying "I can't." You know, the forbidden word.

That sounds harsh, but I don't do it to punish them. I do it to teach them. I tell them, "You can come out of time out when you tell me how to solve your problem." You know what happens? They think up solutions. Sometimes the solutions aren't workable, but they don't just let their circumstances defeat them.

126

The conversation goes something like this:

Lucas: Mom, I can't throw a curve ball.

Me: Sure you can. Give it a try.

Lucas: Mom, I've tried. I can't do it.

Me: Okay, sit in that chair right there until you figure it out.

Lucas (after two minutes): Maybe I just need to practice a little more.

Me: That sounds like a good solution. Do you know what you're doing wrong?

Lucas: No.

Me: Who do you know that might be able to show you?

Lucas: Dad!

Me: Okay. When do you think you can ask him to help you?

Lucas: When he gets home.

Me: Why don't you go out back and practice until then. He'll be back from the store in twenty minutes. Then you can ask him to tell you what you are doing wrong.

Mila once tried to perform a back handspring and couldn't quite get it right. After a few tries, she said, "I can't do it, Mom."

"You have to keep practicing," I told her. "The only way you're going to get better is if you keep doing it over and over again."

It's the same way in real estate, or any business. Shawn and I have had our share of failures. But failures are just a part of the success process. Let your failures drive you. Eventually, with practice, you'll get better at what you're trying to do. We did. Lucas and Mila do. You can too.

A while back, we attended a family ropes course. I've always been afraid of heights, and was on top of this rope climbing platform and looking down. I was up there freaking out, shouting, "I can't do this!"

Mila, bless her heart, looked up and said, "Mom, you can do this! You can do this!" And after the third time of me saying "I can't," she said, "Mom, you shouldn't say that. You're going to time out." She motivated me to complete the course and face my fear of heights. I won because I had her encouragement.

Having someone who can encourage you through the doubts, the fears, and the rough spots is essential. First, I had Grandpa. Now I have Shawn. And Lucas and Mila. You, too, can surround yourself with people who will encourage you. And if you have critics in your life, it's even more important to have people who can encourage you.

Shawn and I became each other's biggest cheerleaders. We encouraged each other when everyone else thought we were playing at a hobby with real estate. That's made all the difference.

Something else that makes a difference is having mentors. I've had a few great friends who mentored me early on. Through the years, Shawn and I have had several mentors help us get through struggles in our real estate business.

Each stage of the business is different, so we outgrew some of the mentors. There's nothing wrong with that. Like the economy, businesses have stages. It's important to change to match the stage of the business. Who I spend time with today is very different than who I hung out with in my twenties. I'm at a different stage in my business, so I have a few different women I like to surround myself with who have good heads on their shoulders. They know what they're doing and have goals in life.

Coaches or mentors can help you get through specific challenges. That is really important in dealing with challenges that friends and family can't help you with.

Another way many people keep themselves from achieving greatness is by limiting themselves. You can have great coaches and mentors, strong encouragers and cheerleaders, and have excellent goals. But if you limit yourself with your self-talk and expectations, you'll rise only so far as your limitations allow.

Finally, it's important not to lose faith. If you believe in God, as I do, then you might consider that He has all things in His hand. He's on control. To me, that means not giving into my fears and letting them control me. It also means that I don't have to be afraid of potential hazards that I can't control.

For the longest time, I was afraid of losing everything that I built. It was so bad that I wouldn't let Shawn spend any money on me. I'd rather put the money in savings than to buy an expensive car, designer clothes, or jewelry. I try to live a simple life, not a luxurious one. But I was so afraid of losing it all, I couldn't allow myself to enjoy what I had. However, I was able to overcome that with the help of a few books and some introspection.

And, of course, God. He taught me to rely on Him. When I realized He can take it all away from me whenever He wants, I gave up trying to control what I can't control. (Appendix 4 has some helpful tips on having a healthy work/life balance.)

Choice Points:

- Surround yourself with encouragers - Whether it's your husband, your children, a co-worker, or a colleague, we all need people in our lives who can encourage us and help us through the challenges. For every critic you have, you should have at least one strong encourager, preferably two.

- Discipline yourself - Success is a choice. It requires discipline. As children, we have parents to discipline us so that we can get on the right track and stay there. As adults, we have to instill discipline in ourselves. Do what it takes to succeed and never give up.

- Success comes down to making good choices- Spend your time on things that matter. Focus on the big picture and the long run instead of giving into instant gratification. Face up to your responsibilities and hold yourself accountable. That means doing the right thing instead of following the path of least resistance. It means stepping out of your comfort zone to face your darkest fears. It also means putting your butt on the line and taking risks when it would be much easier to fall into a safety net. Have the courage to carve your own path.

THE CHOICE IS YOURS: MOM, WIFE, AND CEO

"Think like a queen, a queen is not afraid to fail. Failure is another stepping stone to greatness." — Oprah Winfrey

Thank you for taking this journey with me. It's a personal story. And one that, I hope, has shown there's a path—even from a challenging background like my own (and, perhaps, yours)—through struggle, failure, hard work, and love to a fulfilling and successful life that balances everything you value. And that allows you to be all you want to be as a Mom, Wife, and CEO.

A path based on choice. And Faith. The willingness to fail, learn, and be real with yourself. On self-reliance and the support of the ones you love.

I hope you leave this book with the inspiration to make the changes you want to make and live the life you really want. No matter the odds or challenges. I believe you can. And only you can choose.

If you haven't already, I invite you to keep turning pages to find information you may find helpful in your journey, as well as ways for us to keep connected beyond this book. I'd love to hear about your journey.

Joni

Appendix 1 - Common Fears

All of us have fears. These fears can be motivators or de-motivators. If we allow them to hold us back, we fail to achieve the success we want as wives, moms, and entrepreneurs. Some of the common fears that hold us back include:

Fear of Rejection

The fear of rejection is powerful with a far-reaching impact. Most of us get nervous when we place ourselves in situations that might lead to rejection.

For some people, the fear is crippling. An untreated fear of rejection worsens over time. It gradually takes over every part of your life. To overcome it, you must believe in yourself. You must build your confidence.

To improve self-confidence, you must know where your lack of self-confidence began. Limiting beliefs may stem from events in childhood, often early childhood. If you make them concrete, you can challenge them and they lose their power. Keep a positive and uplifting mental outlook to battle the fear of rejection.

Fear of Socializing

Closely related to the fear of rejection, the fear of socializing is being afraid to interact with others in social settings. It stems from the fear of being judged.

If you have this fear, you'll try to avoid parties and other large events where a lot of people congregate in one place.

People with this fear may find themselves in a crowded room, but they will hide in a corner or avoid interacting with others.

Step out of your comfort zone. People don't bite!

Fear of Failure

Have you ever been so afraid of failing that you didn't try at all? Most of us have experienced this at one time or another.

Fear of failure is immobilizing. When we allow fear to stop our forward progress, we'll miss important opportunities. Fear of failure is often caused by mistakes we've made in our adult lives, but it can also come from devastating childhood experiences.

We all make choices regularly. That includes choosing to be afraid, or not. I was able to overcome fear of failure by setting goals for myself that helped build self-confidence and that challenged me to think positively. If you set small goals for yourself, you'll find yourself moving forward and overcoming your fears.

Fear of Inadequacy

Fear of inadequacy is being afraid you're not good enough. Maybe you're anxious about your skills, education, or your professional value to others. Whatever it is, the fear of inadequacy can grip you and cause you not to perform to the best of your ability. Put it aside and do your best. You are of high value.

Fear of Being Judged

You cannot control what others think of you. Don't worry about what anyone else thinks. Be yourself.

Fear of Losing Everything

Mass media has drilled deep into us the fear of losing everything. We see stories of the rich and famous losing their wealth, or fame. We see stories about good people who lose their health. We see stories about everyday people who lose their homes. Giving in to the fear of losing everything might just cause you to lose everything.

How can you overcome the fear of losing everything?

If you struggle with this fear, you can overcome it by giving some things away. The less you have, the less you fear losing. Let go of the excess, let go of the pride, let go of your love of money, and live for the love of life itself. You can't take your money with you to the grave. The less you fear, the happier you will be and the more success you can enjoy.

In the words of Queen Elsa from the Disney animated film Frozen, "Let it go."

Fear of Losing Anything

Whatever you fear losing, don't hold on too tight. Let it go.

Fear of Losing Your Wealth

Don't be a hoarder. Let it go. You can't take it with you anyway.

Fear of Uncertainty

Uncertainty is a big fear that paralyzes a lot of people. We were all confronted with this one in 2020, weren't we?

Events and situations like stock market crashes and pandemics can create mass uncertainty and mass fear. Don't let it rule you. None of us have control over everything in life. We are not God. There will be uncertainty, and there are very few guarantees in life. Embrace the uncertainty and step out in faith. Just don't be foolish.

Fear of Missing out

Some people are afraid of missing the next big thing. You might be afraid of not achieving a certain level of success, education, or prestige by a certain age. Or you might fear missing out on the next big gold rush.

Here's a news flash: It's okay to miss out on some things. Don't let the fear of missing out destroy your happiness. Some people fear missing out on some things only to let the most important things slip through their fingers. Don't let that be you.

Fear of Change

Change is inevitable. Learn to adapt.

Life is ever evolving. You should prepare for the future, but life is lived one day at a time.

Fear of Losing Control

God is in control and can take anything and everything away from you in an instant.

There will be things in life you can't control. When have you been able to make it rain, or to order sunshine?

You cannot control the economy, the markets, other people, train schedules, and many other things. Learn what you can control and live within those boundaries.

133

Fear of Tragedy

Bad things happen. Tragedy may come at any moment, and it can be powerful. More powerful still is the experience of restoration. When my brother Joey passed, it was tragic, but I was able to find peace within. Overcome tragedy with strength of character. You'll be happier,

Fear of Getting Hurt

The best way to fight the fear of being hurt is to get to know your significant other, or the subject of your fear, on a deeper level. Live your lives together. Allow yourself to be vulnerable.

I had to learn to overcome this fear after my father chose drugs over Joey and me. It hurt, but life went on. Sometimes, being hurt is the life lesson we need.

Fear of Being Authentic or Vulnerable

People who collect big toys often have big egos. They're quick to brag about their possessions. They're also quick to defend their over consumption and self-inflated stories of hard work and success. If you want to defeat any fear of losing, check your ego at the door. Let it go!

Fear can be a huge joy killer. Don't let fear control your life. Use fear to motivate yourself to do better. Overcome fear with courage. Seek out a partner who will hold you accountable, encourage you, and lift you up.

In the words of Franklin Roosevelt, "You have nothing to fear but fear itself."

APPENDIX 2 - INFLUENCES

We all have heroes and sheroes. These are the people with massive influence, and there may even be a small part of yourself who wants to be like them. Whether dead or alive, people of influence can motivate us to be a better version of ourselves.

There are many ways to find people of influence. Reading books and listening to podcasts are two ways modern people find the ideas that influence and motivate them. Some of my own influences include:

- Tony Robbins — He is so motivational. He keeps me focused on all the right things.

- Robert Kiyosaki — Robert Kiyosaki's "Rich Dad, Poor Dad" series of books have been instructional, motivational, and inspirational.

- Ed Mylett — Ed Mylett isn't as well known as Tony Robbins or Robert Kiyosaki, but some day he could be. His podcast The Ed Mylett Show offers straightforward pull-no-punches practical advice for running a business and dealing with fear and obstacles. His guest speakers are as insightful as he is, so the insights gleaned from his podcast have benefited me personally and professionally.

- Rachel Hollis — A female entrepreneur I admire is Rachel Hollis, author of "Girl, Wash Your Face." Her book has been an inspiration to me and has helped me to be more balanced in my approach to running a business while being Mom to my kids and wife to Shawn.

Inspirational Quotes from Top Influencers

"Things may come to those who wait, but only the things left by those who hustle."

— Abraham Lincoln

"Some people dream of success while others wake up and work hard at it."

— Winston Churchill

"You are the average of the five people you spend the most time with."

— Jim Rohn

"You only fail when you stop trying."

— Albert Einstein

"Don't let the sadness of your past and the fear of your future ruin the happiness of your life."

— Source Unknown

"The fact that I was a girl never damaged my ambitions to be a pope or an emperor."

— Willa Cather

"Success depends upon previous preparation, and without such preparation there is sure to be failure."

— Confucius

"Optimism is the faith that leads to achievement. Nothing can be done without hope and confidence."

— Helen Keller

"In the end, we are our choices. Build yourself a great story."

— Jeff Bezos

"Whether you think you can or you think you can't—you're right."

— Henry Ford

APPENDIX 3 - LIVE LIFE TO THE FULLEST

Life is all about choices. We live and die by our choices. No one else can make them for us.

Here are twenty-three steps to living life to the fullest, lessons I learned from my childhood best friend (and a few others along the way):

1. Focus on the present. Yesterday is gone. Tomorrow is still yet to come, so live today to the fullest.

2. Live on the edge. Let challenges drive you. Embrace them to the fullest and expose yourself to new adventures.

3. Keep a journal handy to record your wins in life. Celebrate your wins. Be an inspiration to yourself.

4. Love yourself and love everyone else. Don't look for a reason to love.

5. Accept everyone just the way they are.

6. Be kind and courteous to everyone.

7. Express gratitude.

8. Envy no one. One cannot live life to the fullest when aligned with negativity.

9. Find your purpose in life. Your purpose is the first reason to be alive.

10. Set goals for yourself and be realistic.

11. Practice a more balanced life.

12. Maintain a positive attitude.

13. Be coachable. Be willing to accept criticism and use it to grow.

14. Focus on spirituality. Meditate to rejuvenate and replenish your thoughts.

15. Smile more.

16. Be adaptable, flexible, and open to change.

17. Believe in something

18. Follow your dreams. Write in your journal everything you want to do, pursue them, do not accept defeat.

19. Be yourself and you shall attract the best. Don't worry about what others think of you. You can only control yourself. Master yourself.

20. Do not blame others when you're unhappy. Instead, reflect on yourself and contemplate ways you can be happy.

21. Increase your self-awareness and emotional intelligence.

22. Never stop learning.

23. Be a role model for your children or other young ones who look up to you.

What choices will you make?

You can stick around until the end if that's God's plan for your life, but we are here for just a time. It's a short window. Don't live with regrets.

APPENDIX 4 - HOW TO FIND WORK/LIFE BALANCE

Creating a work/life balance is a necessity for the entrepreneurial wife and mom. You need to draw healthy boundaries between your work life and your family life. The following tips are strategies I implemented to help me manage being a mom, wife, and CEO better with the end goal of creating a healthy work/life balance.

Tip #1: Be a continuous learner.

When Lucas and Mila were born, I committed myself to establishing good personal habits. I read a lot of books during that time to better myself. No matter what stage of life you're in, you must continue to learn. If you aren't learning, you aren't earning.

Tip #2: Encourage your children's independence from an early age.

Both of my kids slept in their own cribs. I believe letting your children sleep with you breeds dependence, and I want mine to grow up to be independent. Lucas and Mila's bed time is private time for Shawn and me. I believe in protecting that time. That's when we connect as a couple. It's important to keep that boundary.

New moms can be afraid. When Lucas was born, I monitored his crib by video all night. I kept the receiver on my bedstand. Every movement Lucas made, I'd run to his room and check on him. It drove Shawn crazy.

In hindsight, it was ridiculous. Now I wonder, what moms did before video monitoring. Their children survived and made to adulthood just fine.

There were times when I almost gave in. One night, Lucas was running a fever. I was tempted to pick him up and carry him back to the bed so he could sleep peacefully between Shawn and me, but Shawn reminded me of our pact. Because he held me accountable, I stayed strong and Lucas remained in his crib.

Whatever expectations you set early in life, you have to deal with the consequences down the road. There's a cause and effect over time, and that brings me to Tip #3.

Tip #3: Set a hard bed time for the children.

Lucas and Mila go to bed at 8:30 p.m. ALL the time. When the hands on the clock hit 8:15, they know it's time to wrap up everything they're doing and ready themselves for a bedtime story. At 8:30, it's momma's time. This is the time I spend with my hubby, the time my massage therapist arrives, the time I take a long quiet bath and listen to music or a podcast, my time to write or do whatever strikes my fancy. I'm in bed by 9:30.

I call this my happy hour and, yes, sometimes it involves a glass or two of Cabernet.

Tip #4: Establish a routine

Routines may sound boring, but I discovered that journaling my day for two weeks was a good starting point.

In your journal, write what you do throughout the day from the time you get up until the time you go to bed. When I started doing this, I was amazed at how I spent my time. There were nine hours each day where I was totally unproductive. At the office and at home. I'd spend hours reading emails and micromanaging employees. No lie, my employees would come into my office and ask questions they should have known the answers to because I'd taught them to be dependent on me.

Once I discovered that I was the world's worst micromanager, I began to allow my employees to discover the solutions to their own problems. That, in turn, improved the efficiency and effectiveness of my business.

Another thing that helped Shawn and me grow the business was taking Fridays off. When we were in the office, that became an excuse for employees to come to us for answers. If we weren't there, they had to figure it out for themselves. And it created more personal time for us.

I also neglected time with my children because I spent evenings answering emails and performing other job-related tasks. That wasn't fair to Lucas and Mila. I quit checking email at home and turned that time into family time.

Taking Fridays off led to Shawn and me taking the family on a month-long vacation. I groomed some handpicked employees to be key leadersand decision-makers in our absence. We systematized every aspect of our business from accounting functions to customer service so that it could run without us. This allowed us to spend a week backpacking in New Mexico, two weeks in Hawaii, and another week in Mexico.

Journaling for two weeks forced me to think about the important things in life. I discovered that work can provide a lifestyle, but it's not the most important thing. If you lose your family and friends, what do you have left?

Tip #5: Set boundaries

Until I started journaling, I was doing well financially. But I felt broken. I knew something had to change.

I wasn't spending enough time with Shawn, Lucas, and Mila. Once I discovered that, I made a list of my priorities. Starting with my life's priorities, I wrote a list of daily priorities based off of them. Next to God, family came first. Then came the other buckets of my life: spirituality, health and fitness, personal development, and work/life balance.

After nailing down my priorities, I began to, spend thirty minutes of quiet time in the morning to give thanks and express gratitude for the things that I have.

Bucket list items

I found that when I spent time in the morning giving thanks to God, my days went better. I also found that when I made time for Shawn, Lucas, and Mila, we had plenty of family time together. Not only did that strengthen our relationships with each other, but it made me more productive in my business.

Another thing, I'm more confident when I feel good about myself. Being physically fit makes me feel good about myself.

When I didn't make fitness a priority, I felt depressed. My demons would tell me I couldn't have a supermodel figure *and* be a terrific mom. But that's a lie! I chose to believe the opposite.

If fitness is important to you, make up your mind to change your priorities.

I'm also a firm believer that, to better yourself, you must be a continuous learner.

I read twenty to thirty minutes every day. My favorite topics are personal development, business development, and being a better parent.

To others, it looks as though I have a pretty awesome life. That's because I've worked hard to create that awesome and balanced life. And it's not just about finances. It's about all areas of my life.

Your choices determine how your life turns out. Planning my days and weeks worked for me. I picked one day of the week to schedule doctor appointments, massages, hair appointments, and other personal items. Friday was that day.

There were Fridays when I didn't have a scheduled appointment, so I focused on personal development.

I use my personal development days to reflect on my goals. Sometimes, they're personal goals. Other times, it involves my business.

Conclusion

I like to read books and listen to podcasts. They teach me a great deal about how to run my business. But good books and podcasts do not always address professional expertise. Sometimes, they're about personal development.

One of my favorite books is "Rich Dad Poor Dad" by Robert Kiyosaki. In fact, Shawn and I liked the book so much we spent our recreational time in college playing the Cashflow board game, based on the same concepts as the Rich Dad Poor Dad books. Instead of "partying" on Friday nights like normal college kids, we'd attend Cashflow events.

I encourage you to develop your own list of books and podcasts that inspire, motivate, and educate you on managing your business and personal life (if you're interested in some of my biggest influences, flip back to Appendix 2 and have a look). They will help you get through the tough times and make the less challenging times more bright and cheery. More importantly, they go along way to helping you achieve a positive work/life balance.

APPENDIX 5: JOURNALING FOR SELF-AWARENESS

You have the ability to write your own story. It doesn't have to be the perfect story, but it can be *your* story. Successful people have a plan. They think about where they want to go, chart a path, and navigate that path with a single-minded vision. Talk to any successful entrepreneur in any business and they'll say the same thing, or something similar: Success is not an accident.

I started thinking more about this the year I was pregnant with Lucas. Prior to that, I worked hard and tried to make as much money as I could while having fun. When I got pregnant, I said to myself, *Joni, you need to figure out why you are doing what you're doing and what the purpose of your life is. How are you going to fulfill your purpose?*

That's when I started journaling.

Through journaling, I discovered some things about myself. Some of it I didn't like! But there were parts of me that were lying dormant and that were valuable parts of who I am. Valuable to others, not just myself.

For instance, I love helping people. I love teaching and sharing how I've navigated certain situations in life. I love seeing people overcome their challenges.

As a result of my journaling, I learned to employ these parts of myself for my employees' benefit. One way I do that is by teaching them how to invest in real estate and implement retirement planning strategies. Instead of offering a 401k plan, I teach them investment strategies through quarterly investment classes and share how directing their own investments can lead to a better retirement plan than an employer-directed plan could do. I've had several employees do quite well. I enjoy watching them succeed.

When planning for life or business, it's best to start with the end in mind. That's something I learned from Stephen Covey, author of *The 7 Habits of Highly Effective People*. If you know where you want to go, it's a lot easier to get there.

Self-awareness is important. Journaling helps to create that self-awareness. But it's not enough. After you become self-aware—encompassing who you are, where you are, and where you want to be—you've got to plan it out. Chart your course. A good place to begin that process is by writing a summary statement, or a vision statement. It doesn't need to be long. Mine was a paragraph. I recommend keeping it shorter than a page.

You can start with a brief summary of what your life looks like right now. After that, write down a few people you look up to—role models, mentors, coaches, successful entrepreneurs—that you can use as a model for your own life. Then, write down your goals and dreams. Where do you want to be in five, ten, and twenty years?

Don't worry about perfection. There is no such thing as the perfect life, perfect vision, or perfect summary statement. You're just thinking about where you want to go from here.

- How will you write your story?

- How will you live your life?

- How will you use your God-given talents?

- What choices will you make to get from Point A to Point B?

- Will you choose a life of ease, or will you choose to live a life full of adventure?

- When life gets tough, will you push through or will you give up the fight?

At the end of the day, every choice is your choice and you are telling your story.

Here's a summary of my story: A little girl wanted more out of life. Despite the crazy obstacles she faced, she managed to develop a vision for life and rise above her circumstances to build two successful businesses. Now she helps others get through their own painful feelings of hopelessness and rejection.

Feeling like an outcast does not have to be the end of your story. For me, it wasn't. I was able to take painful experiences and turn them into a successful career as a mom, a wife, and CEO of my own business. Rather than feel sorry for myself, I focused on how I could succeed by making better choices that benefit my family and me. You can do the same.

Albert Einstein said, "You only fail when you stop trying." Don't stop trying.

APPENDIX 6 - MY DAILY ROUTINE

Here's a little glimpse into my morning routine.

I wake up at 4:30 a.m.

If you wake up early, it means you may have to go to bed earlier. I believe in eight hours of sleep each night. I don't know about you, but when I don't get eight hours of sleep, I'm a hot mess the next morning.

Immediately, when I get up in the morning, I drink an eight ounce glass of water to get myself hydrated. Then I spend fifteen to twenty minutes of quiet time where I pray and give thanks to the Lord. I use that time to foster a spirit of gratitude, and meditate. I then work out for thirty to forty-five minutes. This time starts with a fifteen-minute cardio workout. That wakes me up and gets my blood flowing.

It's difficult to develop the discipline to wake up early in the morning, especially to put yourself through a rigorous workout regimen like I do. However, we all a choice. Remember? You choose what to do with your time. If you feel great about yourself the way you are, awesome! But if you're like me and want to feel better about yourself, then taking care of yourself physically is essential. Where there is a will, there is a way.

I encourage you to add some physical exercise to your daily routine. You can start with one or two days a week if that's what it takes to get going. Working out in the morning not only gives me energy for the rest of the day, but it also makes me feel confident about myself. Thirty minutes of rigorous exercise four to five days a week is a great start.

Three or four days of my week consist of a workout routine my trainer prepped for me. Two days a week consists of some sort of cardio, either spinning or running. That's in addition to the fifteen minute cardio warmup, so I'm effectively getting thirty to forty-five minutes of cardio training on those two days.

I once threw away thousands of dollars on gym memberships and never used them. I always had an excuse. It was too hard, or I didn't have anyone to watch my kids. Shawn got tired of my excuses, so he built a home gym. Now, I go into my garage and work out while the kids are still asleep.

You, too, can create a workout space in your home. It doesn't have to be big. Shawn and I started with a set of dumbbell weights and added to our gym over time.

Videos are also a great way to start. I started with the P90X Beachbody Brazilian Butt Lift. Then I moved on to other video exercise regimes. You name it, I did it.

If you consistently work out three to four days a week, you'll make it a habit. Today, it is a lifestyle for me, and I treat it like daily meal schedules. Working out is a part of my routine. If miss it, I notice.

If you're not used to it, it may seem difficult at first, but if you hang in there long enough, it will become a lifestyle and less of a chore. If you're looking for a starting place, find a sport you like. It could be tennis, swimming, or running. Whatever gets your adrenaline pumping. For me, it's weightlifting. Spinning also gets me fired up.

Another way to stay motivated is to find an accountability partner. I'm not going to lie. There are days when I'm exhausted from work the day before and don't have the motivation to work out. Having Shawn as my accountability partner keeps me on track.

I also have a personal trainer. I check in with her twice a week.

When I don't have a workout plan or routine, I feel lost. It's not fun going to the gym and not knowing what to do, so my trainer prepares my workout plans. She measures me to make sure I'm making progress, and adjusts my plans based on my goals. She also helps me to create a meal plan.

After working out, I have fifteen to twenty minutes before the kids wake up and my day officially starts. I make every minute of my morning ritual count. I take the last fifteen to twenty minutes over a cup of coffee so I can review my plan for the day, make sure my calendar is updated, and to set three priorities for the day. I ask myselfwhat the three most important tasks that need to get done before the end of the day are. These are the three things I put my main focus on that day.

Likewise, I encourage you, as a basic minimum, to create a morning routine. It doesn't matter how the rest of your day goes, if you can conquer the morning and make it yours. When I feel I have conquered half of my day in the morning, the rest of the day belongs to the universe.

Your evening routine is just as important as your morning routine. My goal in the evening is to spend as much time with my family as possible. How is that possible with so many things to accomplish? For me, it starts with meal prepping.

Who has time to cook? With all that I have going on throughout the day, the last thing I want to do is go home and cook after leaving the office. Believe me, I love to cook, but that is not my priority. My priority is spending quality time with my family.

Weekly meal prepping helps. Whether you have someone do it for you or you do it yourself, it's important as a time-saving tool. I've done it both ways. When I did it myself, I prepped my lunches and dinners on Sundays for the beginning of the week. Then, on Wednesday, I prepped the meals for the end of the week. If you love to cook, leave the cooking for the weekends.

I absolutely love to cook. This is the time when I can cater to my family. We make it fun in our household.

Because our time throughout the week is regulated, we use weekends for cooking sprees and make it a family affair. It's amazing, but it's a treat for Lucas and Mila as much as it is for Shawn and me. When we get home in the evenings throughout the week, the meals are already prepped. We eat dinner, do homework, and read twenty minutes together as a family.

A part of our prioritized routine is to read or listen to a daily podcast. If you want to get to the next level, you have to continue learning and improving yourself.

We do it as a family. We set up a library in our home, and every night before bed time we have twenty minutes of quiet time. We sit back, relax on our bean bags, and read our favorite books. It's great, and I encourage you to do this with your children. My kids love it and look forward to our family reading times every night.

Life as a mom, wife, and CEO is not easy. As you can see, it is a balancing act, but I wouldn't have it any other way. It's a choice I made to take on this challenge. Having a daily routine is invaluable.

APPENDIX 7 - TIPS FOR SELF-CARE

Taking care of yourself is an important part of managing your life as mom, wife, and entrepreneur. If you cannot take care of yourself properly, you'll never be able to meet the needs of your husband, your children, your employees, and your customers. Success in life begins with self-care. Therefore, I offer the following tips for the best self-care maintenance:

- Establish a morning self-care routine - Rather than allowing myself to get overwhelmed by trying to catch up on self-care in one day, I've started a regimen of meditation, exercise, and reflection every morning. By making, and taking, time for myself each morning, I get ahead of the stress and keep myself grounded and ready for work each day.

- Reward Yourself - Afford yourself a personal reward from time to time.

- Schedule days off - Adding a day off to my calendar, where I don't let myself schedule any work, has made a major difference for me.

- Get plenty of sleep - I like to sleep at least eight hours every night.

- Moments of gratitude - Reflect on the three best things that happened today. Just before I go to sleep, I write down the three best things that happened that day. This puts me in a state of appreciation and gratitude. Then I ask myself how I could have improved the day. I use these 15 minutes to map out my next day.

- Use positive language and self-talk - One of the most important lessons I've learned is to speak to myself and others positively.

- Make time for family - If you're overloaded with work, many times you'll just head home and crash after the day is done. But it's important to make time for family. It fuels you in a different way.

APPENDIX 8 - EMOTION MANAGEMENT

Putting your emotions in check is not easy, but it is necessary. For me, it's a constant battle. Mental health and awareness is something I continue to work on every day.

As CEO of my own company, I have to be strong mentally. I have to be an example for my employees. If I want to create leaders, I have to be a leader. It doesn't come naturally. It requires hard work, dedication, passion, and the hunger to want it.

Choosing to become a leader will help make your children leaders. My children, from a young age, have seen me work hard. They know what it takes to work hard and to have the lifestyle we enjoy. Your children need to know what it takes to be successful. Too many kids today don't know the value of hard work because their parents never taught them. Choose to be a different kind of parent.

As long as I can balance being a CEO with my personal life, I can have it all and be happy. You can too. Don't let your business run you. Create leaders to help you run your business. Today, I can step away for months and my business will continue to grow because I took the time to train leaders to act in my absence.

The choice to create leaders in my organization to keep it running day to day creates stability in my company. It also establishes stability at home and allows me to live the life I want. This stability allows me to take weeks off at a time to spend with my family, which is the most important thing to me.

There will be a time when your children are grown and would rather spend time with their friends than with you. That's why I want to maximize my time with Lucas and Mila right now and live my life with no regrets.

You, too, can create a life with no regrets. The choice is yours!

My advice to you is to never stop dreaming. When you have fulfilled your dreams and reached your goals, set new dreams and higher goals. Often, when we achieve a dream or a goal, we hit a wall and stop dreaming. That, my friends, is when you lose your passion for life. I've been guilty of this myself. But I've been able to accomplish every dream and goal I've set for myself.

At one point, I had achieved everything I wanted. I stopped dreaming. I was lost. I didn't know what else to do, or what my next dream was. I had no new goals to set. I had to outgrow my circle of influence to get to the next level. I had outgrown my peers. It's not that we don't talk today, but in order to get to the next level of thinking, I had to interact with peers above my level. That was hard. I had say "No" to my old friends many times when they wanted to go out and do things with me. Today, my priorities are very different than they were a year or two ago. And it started with a choice.

You can be content with where you are today, or, you can grow. You may have to make some difficult decisions, but growth doesn't come from stagnation.

The last piece of advice I can give you is this: Don't dwell on the past. We all have a past, and, as you can see, my past involved horrific events. What I learned was, there are events that will happen which are out of our control. Family drama will be there. It is how you react to these events that matters. You can choose.

You can have pity on yourself and beat yourself up, or you can use challenges to your advantage. Let them build you up and make you stronger. You can prove to yourself that you can do it. Who cares what everyone else thinks? It is not their life. It is *your* life you are living.Make it a life that you won't regret.

We ladies are capable of handling anything as long as we are aware of where we need to put our energies. And we must have a strong belief in ourselves. It is this belief that helps us manage our emotions and keeps us mentally healthy to perform.

ACKNOWLEDGMENTS

I'd like to acknowledge the following people in my life without whom this book could not have been written:

- My husband Shawn Wolfswinkel. He is my rock, my biggest supporter, and the one who encouraged me to tell my story.

- My mother, who taught me many life lessons, including the value of hard work, and showed me what it means to never give up.

- My grandfather, who adored me, taught me about life, and raised me to be a humble but strong independent woman.

- My grandmother, who loved me unconditionally by raising me as one of her own.

- My stepdad. He loved my mother, treated her with respect, and took on the immense responsibility of raising me to be the woman I am today.

- My staff, client, and vendors. They keep the wheels of my business spinning.

And a big thank you to you, dear reader, for taking the time to enjoy this journey with me. You humble me and encourage me to make the world a better place. I hope you'll find some inspiration and motivation in these pages to propel you and your career, as well as your status as mom and wife, to higher highs and greater achievements. I invite you to listen to my podcast titled Inside the Wolf's Den at Spotify and the Apple iStore and YouTube. Also connect with me on social media at the following venues:

Jonimwolf (@jonimwolf) • Instagram photos and videos

Joni Wolfswinkel | Facebook

About Joni Wolfswinkel

 Joni Wolfswinkel is an accomplished business leader with more than twenty years in the trenches. She writes and speaks about women empowerment and encourages women entrepreneurs around the world to seek self-development and personal growth. As CEO of Real Property Management Preferred, she was listed among the top 100 women of influence in leadership within the housing industry by HousingWire for the year 2020.

A devoted wife and mother, she is also recognized as a top producing real estate agent, CEO of three different franchises, owner of a nationally recognized investment property firm, and owner of a leading virtual assistant supplier company.

Joni spearheads the successful entrepreneurial podcast, "Inside The Wolf's Den" with her husband Shawn.

Outside of the office, Joni is persistent in her dedication to servant leadership. She serves on the board of directors for the Bridge the Gaps Foundation, a non-profit organization that assists underprivileged, low-income, and at-risk athletic students. She and her family also sponsor special needs children through the Lenn Foundation and have spent several years volunteering with Generous Genius.

Joni Wolfswinkel lives in Houston, Texas, with the "Wolfpack," made up of herself, Shawn, and their children Mila and Lucas.